Let's talk about BF

Strategies, Skills and Stories to change minds and defend yourself against the dark Brexit arts

We seek a Better Britain in a Better Europe
for a Better World

Peter Cook

Why I wrote this book

I am of a certain age. Speaking personally, Brexit will not affect me positively or negatively. I'm pretty sure I'll be in a shallow grave by the time that any of the supposed Brexit benefits materialise. Even 18th Century retro imperialist faux gent Jacob Rees-Mogg said that we will get nothing back from Brexit for 50 years ... I'm impatient at my age ...

We are merely responsible landlords of planet earth. If we do well in our lives, we leave the planet in a better state that when we arrived. But we must at least be guided by the principle of "do no harm." We owe it to our children, their kids and the planet to do our best and stand up to those who would do harm in pursuit of narrower and more destructive goals. This requires us to continue the conversation with leave voters, sometimes against difficult odds. Let's talk about BREX .. it will equip you with strategies, skills and stories to help you have these difficult conversations.

Human beings have achieved great things for the planet. Sadly the human condition also includes a few human faults. Greed, avarice, ego and so on. It means we think short term, sometimes selfishly and nostalgically. Crucially we don't always have a systemic view of our neighbours and others we share this fragile earth with. As far as I know, earthworms, hydrangeas and molluscs do not share the faults of the "human race." It is perhaps time to stop racing and consider what we can learn from the rest of the animal and plant kingdom. After all, we are allegedly more intelligent than snails ...

Brexit is, at one level, a gross example of selfishness, greed and avarice by a few disaster capitalists. These people have successfully persuaded the masses that Brexit will be good for them. The Dunning Kruger effect and misplaced pride prevent some leave voters from admitting that Brexit will not deliver any of the supposed benefits we were mis-sold so compellingly. This plays out daily via snappy catchphrases such as "Take Back Control", "Brexit Means Brexit", "Enough is Enough" etc. Feelings overwhelm facts in the tsunami of data that arrives daily across our TV screens, computers and smartphones. Senses working overtime.

Let's talk about BREX .. it

The information age is in part responsible for the Brexit vote. Aside from interference in the voting process by Cambridge Analytica, another effect is in play here. We receive some 34 GB of data daily. This more than the average person received in their entire life in 1800. Quite naturally the response to "drowning in data" in some cases is to shut down from information overload. Nigel Farage understood this well, when he asked the nation to vote with their hearts and not their heads after we were numbed senseless by data.

I originally titled this book "The Brexit Monologues." Why a monologue I hear you say? Surely a conversation is a dialogue? Well some of the conversations I've had with some hardcore leave voters have been monologues. In other words they simply wish to unload their "story" on me before there is any possibility of a dialogue. I have had literally thousands of conversations with Brexiteers in cafés, bars and on the street. Listening skills do not arise until I have invested sufficient time and energy in understanding their viewpoints, however much I may disagree with them. Why exactly should they wish to listen to me anyway? Many of them simply want to download their concerns, issues and fantasies about Brexit and their feelings of being left behind. In listening to these people I have found that their monologues are actually quite revealing. At the same time, some level of therapy can occur by simply allowing these people to vent their feelings of rage, disappointment, and regret about their lives. Occasionally, it is possible to separate their feelings from the causes of these feelings. In other words to separate their regrets from the fact that the EU is not the root cause of their regrets. Once we have achieved that we have the possibility for what I call in a slightly tongue in cheek way a "Brexorcism."

Let's talk about BREX .. it provides strategies, skills and stories to help you conduct your own Brexorcisms whilst helping you to look after yourselves in the process. I use the word Brexorcism not because I'm expecting you to throw holy water at your subjects. Nor do I expect you to have to deal with people whose heads and viewpoints rotate 360 degrees. We are generally dealing with quasi-religious beliefs or even identity level change, where Brexit is intimately linked with people's sense of self. We are sometimes seeking to challenge people at the level of who they are or the why of their being. This requires skill, time and flexibility on our part.

This book is not just about Brexit ghostbusting. Where Brexit leads, Trump, Erdogan and others follow. Just as sure as ladies' hemlines rise and fall for no particular reason with the whims of fashion every year, populism is also a fashion statement that others follow. So, you will find this book of immense value if you are trying to fight populism anywhere in the world.

Let's talk about BREX .. it

On New Year's Day 2017 I coined the catchphrase "Break Brexit Before Brexit Breaks Britain." I note this has been adopted and adapted quite widely. I recently realised that it needed updating. On New Year's Day 2019 I came up with a new mantra which may need to be shortened if we manage to organise a Live Aid styled concert to stop Brexit populism with pop music this year.

"We seek a Better Britain

in a Better Europe

for a Better World."

We are all in this together and it is about time we woke up to the fact.

I hope this gives some clues as to why you might want to read this book ... read on ...

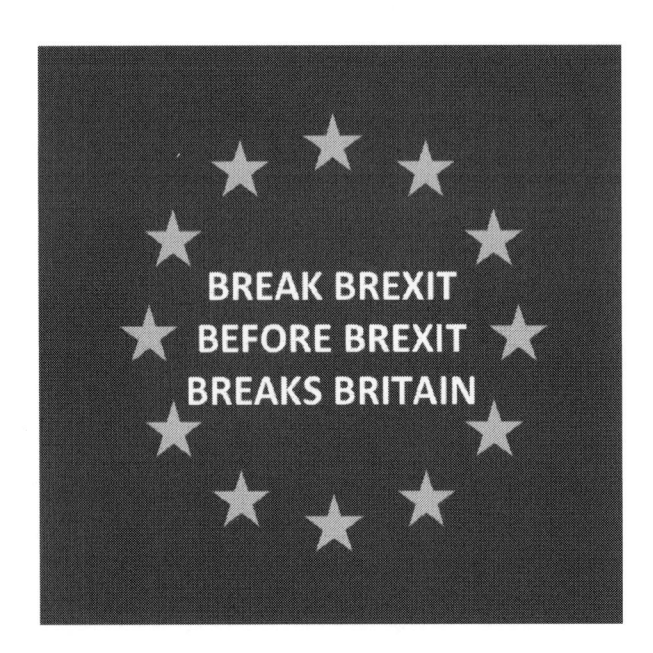

Why you should read this book

We have reached a point of what I call "Brexit Apathy" on both sides of the false binary debate that has atomised our United Kingdom. Brexit voters are rightly tired of Remainiacs, proselytising, cajoling, shouting, singing. In some cases they attempt to hug Brexit supporters to death, "killing them with kindness, understanding and warm fuzzies." By the same token, some Remainers are also unimpressed with the ongoing tsunami of Brexit resistance, as active protest is not the "English" way. Some Remain supporters are now paradoxically of the view that we must follow the "will of the people", especially if that avoids civil unrest.

My brother is a case in point. He voted Remain but now exhibits what academics call "learned helplessness." In other words, he does not know what he could do to change the course of history. Nor does he believe he has the right to interfere with the will of the people. He also fears street violence. This in spite of the fact that the evidence suggests that the vast majority of people have fallen asleep about Brexit. Some even believe we have already done Brexit in my area of "Brexit Central."

You will find Let's talk about BREX .. it of value if you want to know how to:

- Deal with Brexit apathy on both sides of the binary debate to change minds such that we stop the rush into Brexit self-harm.

- Overcome the sheer despair of offering reasoned debate to leave voters, only to be shouted at with such platitudes as "Get Over It – We won – 2-Nil – End Off."

- Cope with verbally and physically aggressive leave voters in their attempt to silence democracy. I myself was punched in the face, receiving two black eyes, by 7 people who had run out of words to conduct a dialogue and found it easier to use fists as an instrument of persuasion. If you are to conduct what I call "Brexorcisms" we must expect aggressive reactions at times, although physical violence is very much an exception.

- Win the battle for hearts and minds in populist media.

- Heal strained relationships with friends and family after Brexit, at home, on the streets and on social media.

- Ride the roller coaster of personal emotions that Brexit uncertainty has thrown at us – what J.K. Rowling would call "Defence Against the Dark Brexit Arts."

In this book, I've set out strategies, tools and techniques that I and others have used over nearly three years of almost full-time anti-Brexit activism. They are illustrated with stories that give example as to how to turn around some of the most closed minds on the subject. I have done this in the hope that these will offer some inspiration and support to others. Of course, not everyone can be converted. I've also included some examples of "glorious failures", in case you can find alternative strategies that work. Sometimes failure is a better teacher than success. In the end, all such work is highly situation dependent. Just because something does not work in one circumstance does not mean it won't work in a different situation.

These approaches are of value whether we cancel Brexit in the coming months or not. If Brexit ends, there will be much healing of relationships to be done. In the event of a People's Vote, there will also be much influence and persuasion to be done. This book will also be of use in any of the theatres of populism that are sweeping the world. For example, Trump's America and other places where grass roots activism is needed to establish healthier approaches to politics and civil societies.

Some of what follows is sublime. In other cases, the stories verge on the ridiculous. I have tried not to be too serious in putting these stories together as humour oils the imagination. However, I'm deadly serious about having fun whilst defending yourself against the dark Brexit arts and conducting what I have named "Brexorcisms." In other words, undoing embedded quasi-religious beliefs about Brexit, associated myths and legends.

Are you ready for some Brexit ghostbusting?

Dedication

To my two sons Thomas and James. May you live to see the end of Brexit. Having excelled at learning you are equipped to ride the storm whatever happens. Wishing you every happiness for a more enlightened world.

To my wife Alison, who has put up with nearly three wasted years of Brexit nonsense from our Government with patience, grace and support, all my love.

To my mother in law Eileen, who always put her grandchildren first and who recently passed away. Unlike many older people, she voted to Remain in the EU so that her grandchildren could enjoy the freedoms afforded by our membership of the European Union. May you rest in peace in the knowledge that you left the world a better place for your presence.

To all that campaign in small or larger ways to build a Better Britain in a Better Europe for a Better World, you are the true patriots in this peculiar adventure.

Grateful thanks to Alison Murray for being a constant source of inspiration towards the completion of this book.

The Brexit Monologues

PART I – Strategies

I.	How will Brexit end?	11
II.	Let's talk about BREX .. it	24
III.	Defence Against the Dark Brexit Arts	42
IV.	It ain't what you do, it's the way that you do it	62
V.	Mind your language	77

PART II – Skills and Stories

I.	Dance, Music, Sex, Romance … and Brexit	102
II.	Brexit Oddity	105
III.	Isas, Isis and Brexit	110
IV.	Suffer Little Children	111
V.	No wonder you're fed up	113
VI.	The Brexit punch bowl	115
VII.	Political Correctness and Brexorcism	120
VIII.	Money, Money, Money	121
IX.	Yellow Vests	125
X.	The Immigrant Song	127
XI.	Are you a Citizen of Nowhere?	128
XII.	Trumptown and Brexit	133

XIII.	Tennis Elbowed	135
XIV.	A Fisherman's tail	137
XV.	Let's write about Brexit	139
XVI.	Spooking out your MP	143
XVII.	An Unhealthy Brexit	148
XVIII.	The Smiths	153
XIX.	Late night, Maudlin Street	154
XX.	Brief Encounters of the 3rd kind	156
XXI.	To the Brexit Manor Born	158

Part III – Defence Against the Dark Brexit Arts

Defence Against the Dark Brexit Arts	160
Reasons to be cheerful	170
Useful links	188

Let's talk about BREX .. it

PART I

Strategies

Chapter I
How will Brexit end?

Before setting out in search of strategies, skills and stories to defeat Brexit populism, let's talk about why and how Brexit will end sooner or later. What follows is essentially a prologue which addresses the "why" question. Why we must continue to resist any sub-standard Brexit and persuade others of the folly of capitulation through apathy and confusion.

The DisUnited States of Brexitania

It is just weeks away from our scheduled date of leaving the European Union. In nearly three years since our referendum it has become apparent that:

1. There remain no detailed plans for Brexit. All the sketchy plans for Brexit (Chequers, No Deal etc.) are inferior to the deal we currently have with the EU. The various works of fiction such as Canada ++++, Norway special, Carlsberg Special, Jobs, Jobsworth, Green, Green Day, Red, Red Wedge, White, White Stripes Blue, Blue Monday, Black, Black Friday or any of the other "50 shades of Brexit" have zero substance. What my wife calls "Fur Coat, No Knickers" Brexit deals.
2. There remain no answers to the question "How will Brexit benefit me or the country?" Even former UKIP leader Nigel Farage cannot answer the question, preferring to blame the Greek philosophers for Brexit. I discovered this recently in his reply to my question within an article I provided to The Independent newspaper. The subject also came up in a panel session with Vote Leave and Open Britain on LBC with Iain Dale. Also, when I called Nigel on his radio show, disguised as an unemployed merchant banker from Hackney named David …

Nigel Farage's office tells constituent his degrees are 'pointless' after he raises questions about Brexit

Exclusive: Peter Cook says he feels 'very insulted' after the exchange

Shehab Khan | @ShehabKhan | Tuesday 28 August 2018 18:00 |
1.3K shares | 274 comments

3. There remains confusion about what Brexit means due to the "50 Shades" problem. However, it has become clearer that Brexit offers no value economically, socially, environmentally, ethically and so on, when compared with our current membership of the EU. This costs us 37 pence a day, or half a Mars Bar, for 70 + years of overall peace in Europe. Jacob Rees-Mogg's best estimate of 50 years "Net Present Value" for Brexit will see my sons aged 75 and 72 by the time Brexit is likely to "break-even." Thomas and James will be paying for Brexit for all of their adult lives due to our fence-sitting behaviour and English complacency. It is not a legacy I want on my tombstone. How about you?
4. It becomes clearer with every day that passes that Brexit is simply the pursuit of a political ideology for the few, not the many. All challenges to Brexit, be they legal, technical, social or otherwise have been ignored by our Government and the official opposition. They have put their parties before the good of the country and its people.

Some say that Brexit cannot be stopped. They include my own brother. They are wrong. They merely demonstrate the condition psychologists call "learned helplessness." This occurs when people do not believe they can or should affect the outcome of an event and / or they don't know what to do about it to alter the course of events. In my brother's case he tells me that, although he voted to Remain, he believes it would be undemocratic to go against the "will of the people." He knows that Brexit will be bad for him and his family but believes we must keep calm and carry on. This deeply "English" condition is a powerful force in allowing bad things to happen. Fear from the "silent majority" was also a feature of Hitler's rise to power. We must not repeat this mistake.

Brexit Chaos

Brexit is very likely to end, sooner or later, through the chaotic combination of a number of countervailing forces. I've summarised some of these in this series of "event strings" below. Different combinations of events lead to a number of end game Brexit scenarios. Some of these are a slow painful death of the Brexit beast. Others more rapid in nature. All the end game scenarios are precarious but not as dangerous as continuing with Brexit. I'm quite sure that events and their combined effects will have changed to some degree by the time that I publish this book, as Government strategy changes almost daily. Time will tell …

Brexit Realities

"Of course, Brexit means that something is wrong in Europe. But Brexit means also that something was wrong in Britain."

Jean Claude Junker

"An Englishman, a Scotsman and an Irishman walk into a bar. The Englishman wanted to go so they all had to leave."

Anon

Let's talk about BREX .. it

Macro effect	Possible Event Strings
External shock	The EU rejects continuing attempts to negotiate "cake and eat it deals." This is due to fundamental lack of progress on the 20% of the issues the cause 80% of the difficulty in squaring the Brexit circle. For example, Northern Ireland, EU Citizen's rights, freedom of movement etc. Parliament comes to its senses and suspends Article 50. The UK opts for No Deal Brexit. Civil unrest occurs as food and medicine shortages hit the population. Britain becomes an unsafe place for a few weeks until the Government withdraws Article 50 in a humiliating defeat of imperialist thinking. The EU lets us re-join but we never regain our privileged position within Europe. The Government falls. A well-timed combination of other issues brings Brexit to an abrupt end e.g. the myriad number of legal challenges, Northern Ireland backstop stasis, Gibraltar, The Falklands, Industry pressure on trade and freedom of movement and so on.
Internal Combustion	The civil service continues to work with the inherent complexity / wickedness of the details of Brexit until a point of entropy or stasis arises. The Conservative and / or Labour Parties melt down to the point where a general election and / or leadership contest arises. This is fought along the lines of "To Brexit or Remain." A coalition of former Prime Ministers stand firm in the centre to promote tactical voting to the point of no overall control. Other surprising outcomes arise for parties that support a Better Britain in a Better Europe for a Better World.

Internal Combustion **(Cont'd)**	Theresa May sees that the only way to save her party and reunite the country is to call an advisory People's vote as a "blessing" on a Parliamentary vote to withdraw Article 50. She secures a mandate to limp on to the next election and put Brexit behind her. As a result, her reputation increases beyond measure as the woman who saved Britain, her party and Europe. Parliamentary paralysis continues, leading to civil disruption and an opportunity for the centre to unite in a people's coalition to end Brexit. A mature form of populism emerges in Britain. The people begin to organise in ways that make traditional politics and Westminster irrelevant.

These events are by no means the only ones possible and the number of combinations endless. Use the above table to stimulate your own thinking on what may happen. Record your thoughts about the issues in the grid below:

Thinking about Brexorcism

Questions	My thoughts
How do you think Brexit will end?	
If it does not, what will the implications be? Short-term Longer-term	

Learned helplessness

The condition when people do not believe they **can** or **should** affect the outcome of an event.

They also don't know what they **could** do about it to alter the outcome.

Brexit end game scenarios

In my work as a business consultant, I've used scenario planning as a "gaming" technique. In particular, to help companies such as Johnson and Johnson and Pfizer anticipate and respond to alternative futures. Scenario Planning was popularised by Royal Dutch Shell in the 1970's. Shell was widely regarded as being ahead of its time in helping others to understand complexity and uncertainty.

A fortuitous meeting with Vince Cable re-ignited my enthusiasm to think about some of the more likely combinations of events that could lead to the death of the Brexit beast. Vince was an ex Shell employee and fellow scenario planner. He and I agreed that it was probably impossible to game all the possible permutations. However, it was at least possible to consider the end coming, in either one of three directions:

1. Internal combustion, put crudely, "heat without light", or;
2. From a combination of external shocks;
3. More likely, a combination of both internal and external effects.

We are in disruptive times. Linear planning perspectives no longer apply. Just consider these examples that illustrate the unlikely, unwitting and criminally insane approaches of our Government in recent times:

- How unlikely it was that Theresa May would "get into bed" with the DUP?
- Who knew that she would expect the taxpayer to fund the cost of stockpiling food, drugs and fuel as a strategy to frighten the country into submission and as a "game of chicken" with Michel Barnier?
- Who would have predicted that our Government would expect people to exist on a what has euphemistically been called a "reduced diet" to get us through a No Deal Brexit? Will Pease Pudding and Marrowfat Peas become gentrified as a national favourite dish on Jamie Oliver soon?
- Who could have foreseen that our Government would engage a shipping company with no ships to reassure us about transport of food and medicines?

Here is some future gazing taken from the event strings. The one thing we know about the future is that it is unreliable. At the time of writing we seem to be still on the general trajectory towards a meltdown of the Conservative party. Sajid Javid is attempting to save the party for 125 000 pensioners, who will eventually exhale their last bad Brexit breaths on their Brexit beds. This moment is also quite dangerous in terms of the disruptive and desperate strategies that people and groups attempt in such times.

The EU have kept their powder dry for nearly three years of Brexit negotiations. They have consistently had to endure endless repackaging of the "cake and eat it too" proposals. "Cakeism" characterises UK Government hubris about empire and other historical and hysterical notions of a lost paradise.

The EU have now stated that the time for further negotiation is over. Should Theresa May now attempt to come up with more "old wine in new bottles", I predict that there will be a hardening of attitudes in Brussels to further obfuscation. An outright rejection of our proposals will not be an act of belligerence on the part of the EU. Quite simply, if the EU were to give Britain a special deal, it would open the floodgates in terms of other countries asking for similar treatment. What exactly would be the point of being an EU member when you could gain similar concessions without paying the club membership fees?

I consider "No Deal Brexit" to be a low probability overall, especially after recent events. It could only really come about if we somehow timed ourselves out at the time of writing. No Deal would guarantee that the Conservative party would be unelectable into perpetuity. However, it is an incredibly potent way of silencing resistance … if we fall for it. The effects are unimaginable, with deaths related to medicine shortages likely. I won't detail them here as they are adequately covered in the chapter entitled "Who Cares About Brexit." Suffice to say that, considering the near hysteria that occurred when KFC ran out of chicken, there is a real possibility of civil unrest within days of a No Deal Brexit. I do not believe that the rank and file Conservative MPs are self-harmers. We must not confuse an attempt to bludgeon the nation and the EU into acceptance of a sub-standard Brexit deal with a serious intent to "Make Conservatives History" via No Deal.

Never underestimate the importance of entropy in extinguishing a political strategy. This is the stuff on which "Yes Minister" was based. The stoic efforts of our civil service work quietly but consistently to place obstacles in the way of Brexit. I've had many private conversations with individuals in high and low places who tell me such things …

I also talk a lot with people on social media on both sides of the Brexit dilemma. There is dismay on both sides about the lack of progress being made. Meanwhile the rhetoric continues to say that the "Brexit Titanic" has left the harbour and it will be plain sailing ahead. I am always much more interested in what is happening in politics behind the stage than on stage. Private conversations with people who face the politicians on a

Brexitosis

A delusional condition. If left untreated it can lead to FBFR (**F**ull **B**lown **F**ar **R**age), characterised by statements such as:

"We need them more than they need us."

"We can have our cake and eat it too."

"The EU are going to tell us what type of toilet roll we can use."

"There are two million rapists waiting to invade Tonbridge from Berlin."

Let's talk about BREX .. it

daily basis via the "Stand of Defiance European Movement" or SODEM indicate that the Brexit process is not plain sailing at all. This means that further defections, resignations, revolts and so on will continue, further weakening the "Brexit Obsessive Compulsive Disorder" to breaking point. We have already seen Boris Johnson starting disruptive operations in the Conservative Party and similar movements are taking place to the left. Movements in the centre may suddenly make it a more attractive place to be …

Others see things differently. Eminent business consultant William Buist outlines a pathway to a Government of national unity here. Time will tell as to what really happens …

1. Theresa May loses the parliamentary vote.
2. She puts an ultimatum vote to parliament of going for no deal and loses that too, but by a slimmer margin.
3. Jeremy Corbyn calls a vote of no confidence. January has now passed.
4. Theresa May wins, but only just. She resigns.
5. The Conservatives try to form a government but fail.
6. Jeremy Corbyn tries to form a government but fails. February is gone.
7. We can't have a General Election, there's no time for a People's Vote. The Queen invites someone like Caroline Lucas, or a Cross-bench Lord to form a Government of national unity. They get sufficient temporary commons support for that by committing to a two-year long reconciliation process. This requires rescinding Article 50 and setting in train a national consultation on a "Vision for Britain". They commit to a referendum on that vision three months before the next General Election.

How Brexit Ends

Through deliberate or accidental seismic combinations of:

External Events

Internal Obstacles

"Jacob Rees-Mogg seeks an "erotic spasm" for the hardest possible break from the EU."

This is the end my friends

It is never a good idea to pursue a strategy in the face of compelling evidence that it will not deliver a better future. All good business people know this and so do most serious politicians. The present difficulty for Theresa May and her Government is how to stop Brexit **AND** remain electable. A change to the "parliamentary paralysis" that has locked Britain in a state of political entropy can come from a combination of actions on our part. Here's my "Five A Day." What are yours?

1. Continue to explain the benefits of EU membership. Debunk items labelled project fear as Brexit reality. Many of the effects branded "Project Fear" have already come to pass or are now starting to materialise. It is becoming clearer that nobody voted to make themselves poorer or have fewer rights.

2. Challenge misconceptions that continue to occupy the minds of leave voters, sometimes sensitively, sometimes provocatively, depending on the person / group involved. We will turn to these in subsequent chapters.

3. Keep asking your MP to have courage, in some cases, to begin growing a spine. Point out gently or otherwise that they are unelectable if they do not stand up for the best interests of the country. It is actually written into their job description so we are really just asking them to do their job.

4. Keep talking about the state of play and the fact that Brexit can be stopped. Speak with friends, family, colleagues, burnt out Remainers, Leavers in regret, Leavers in denial etc. to target the issue of learned helplessness.

5. March and get active locally in whatever way you can. Never let a day pass without doing something to "Break Brexit Before Brexit Breaks Britain."

The rest of this book deals with the slow but steady work of personal influence and persuasion needed to achieve your five a day.

Thinking about Brexorcism: My Five a Day

Element	My applications
1. Continue to explain the benefits of EU membership. Debunk items labelled project fear as Brexit reality.	
2. Challenge misconceptions that continue to occupy the minds of leave voters, sometimes sensitively, sometimes provocatively, depending on the person / group involved.	
3. Keep asking your MP to have courage, in some cases to begin growing a spine. Point out gently or otherwise that they are unelectable if they do not stand up for the best interests of the country.	
4. Talk about the state of play and the fact that Brexit can be stopped, to friends, family, colleagues, burnt out Remainers, Leavers in regret, Leavers in denial etc.	
5. March and get active locally in whatever way you can. Never let a day pass without doing something to "Break Brexit Before Brexit Breaks Britain."	

Chapter II
Let's talk about BREX .. it

This chapter concerns the gentle art of influence and persuasion. This is what we must do to change hearts, minds and souls on Brexit. People have their own preferred ways of being persuasive. I've noticed over nearly three years of working on the street with grass roots Remain campaigners that there is a preference for what I call "push marketing" methods as the weapon of choice. These approaches manifest themselves in placards, chants, songs and other forms of "telling" the other side to reform their minds. There's nothing wrong with these as a means of mass communication. Even I have had my moments at doing such things, on the street at No 10 Downing Street and via our song projects at "Rage Against the Brexit Machine" www.brexitrage.com However, there are many other styles. Arguably some of the less demonstrative ones are better in terms of influence and persuasion when the subject of your attention already has strongly formed views. So, we begin with an overview of the anatomy of influential communications.

Communications and influence

We live in an increasingly fragmented and busy world, with many competing activities and stimuli for our attention, time and money. Compared with 50 years ago, we have multiplied the number of ways we can communicate. These provide certain freedoms to live spontaneously. For example, we can literally live in a "Last Minute" economy. Yet, more communication devices and faster communications do not always make for better communications when careful planning is needed, as opportunity is missed.

Success in communications can be reduced to four elements:

Communication summed up in one minute

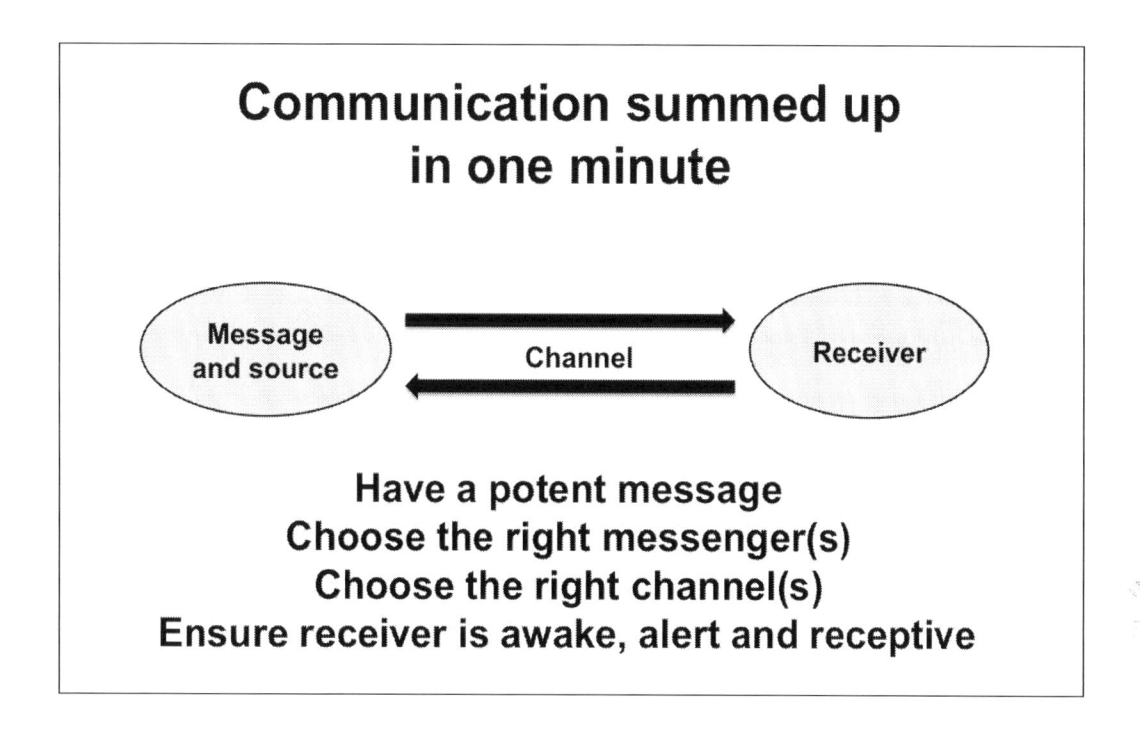

Message and source ⇄ Channel ⇄ Receiver

Have a potent message
Choose the right messenger(s)
Choose the right channel(s)
Ensure receiver is awake, alert and receptive

1. The Message

Successful communicators use very clear, potent messages to engage and coalesce people around a goal or a project. Fuzzy messages drive fuzzy actions and fuzzy outcomes. In short, fail to plan, plan to fail.

Applying this to the EU referendum, it becomes clear as to why people believed the message that we could spend £350 million per week on our NHS instead of the EU by "taking back control." Although the message proved to be false and was retracted the day after the vote had been cast, this did not matter to people who wanted to believe the message. Irrespective of your views on the matter, it was an undeniably clear and potent message. It was carefully calculated to create what academics call "order control certainty" in the minds of voters. It could have only been improved by making it seem to be a calculated number by using something like £357 million.

The notion of "taking back control" has since proved to be a **nominalisation** in linguistic terms. Nominalisation is the process of turning a word from a verb into a noun. It has become painfully clear that people did not realise what they were taking back control of, when, where and so on. For example, if we leave the EU we will no longer be able to send refugees back to Europe, an unintended consequence of leaving the bloc.

Research on communications also has wide implications for those of us who aim to undertake Brexorcisms. Consider carefully these insights:

1. Firstly, let us consider the issue of one-sided versus two-sided messages. One-sided messages work best when the receivers already agree with the argument, or when they are unlikely to hear counter arguments. This may explain why people read newspapers that already accord with their views. It clearly worked with our example of the £350 million for the NHS. This rather demonstrates that we are essentially in echo chambers for much of the time. In other words, we are only ever confronted with views that we are already consonant with.

   Two-sided messages tend to be more effective when the receivers initially disagree with the argument, where they are well educated, or when they are likely to hear counter arguments from others. The ramifications of this innocent sounding sound bite are massive in terms of thinking about your choice of persuasive communications. Many of us do not like to appear to argue away from our preference, yet it can be very effective when trying to see things from a Brexiteer's viewpoint. For example, I know many people who loathe Boris Johnson so much that they could not bring themselves to agree with anything he says, even if they actually agree with it. I'd go so far to say that the ability to argue from multiple viewpoints separates the sheep from the goats in terms of influence. This example from the street demonstrates the wisdom of seeing things from the both sides:

We're in the Army now

I was talking to three people who turned out to be Vote Leave professionals on Parliament Square. They assumed me to be of low intelligence initially as I had my F...CK Brexit T-Shirts, my hi-vis orange jacket and my anti-Brexit hoardings on my bicycle. I therefore looked more like the gasman than a business academic! I, in turn, thought that my "opponents" were Remainers, as they were at the daily SODEM protest.

We're in the Army now

We started as if we were having some kind of casual chat, which turned out to be a massive advantage. Within a few minutes, it became apparent that they voted to leave the EU and worked at Millbank at Vote Leave HQ.

They started to rehearse the usual set of Vote Leave issues such as the EU Army, unaccountable bureaucracy and a host of other concerns they had. I answered all the issues raised politely and each one with evidence. On some issues I conceded that they had a point. They were very surprised when I pointed out that the EU needed reform, as did all political systems. The army dialogue was most interesting:

Vote Leave: "Are you not concerned about an EU army?"

Me: "Not really. Despite my appearance as a bit of a yob, I used to tutor MBA students and am in my "cycling wear" today. I have had a lot of senior army people on my MBA programme over the years. One told me that joining an EU army would be pretty good idea for two reasons:

- Firstly, as one of the most experienced armies the British Army would likely be at the head of an EU Army.
- British soldiers in the EU army would also be properly resourced, unlike the British Army.

Setting aside false notions of union flags, Queen and country my army guy pointed out that an EU Army is a pretty good idea ..."

They did not challenge this. After we finished talking, they complimented me, saying that they had never had such a reasonable conversation with a Remainer at Parliament. Although I could not have possibly converted them, we shook hands and there was mutual respect in our exchange.

Ask yourself: When will a two-sided approach be best? When is it right to go for the one-sided approach?

2. When communicating to persuade, it is generally better to draw a conclusion in the message rather than letting others attempt to infer it themselves. By not drawing a conclusion we invite the possibility that a different one may be drawn. Or, that no conclusion will be drawn from the passive supply of information. When thinking about persuading leave voters of your viewpoint, it is always be better if they drew the conclusions themselves. People much prefer their own thinking than that of others. However, if there is a risk of them drawing a different conclusion, drive your point home with a conclusion and then deal with objections. A typical example would be when saying that the Brexit on offer is not the one offered in the "brochure" in 2016. This is typically met with the objection "that's because the EU have bullied us" or "you traitors have brought the country to its knees".

3. Repetition of a message can increase persuasiveness if used cleverly. However, over-repetition can wear out a message as well. Just note how many people have become irritated by the phrases "Strong and Stable", "Deep and special partnership" and "Brexit means Brexit" for a graphic illustration of how a robotic approach offends many. Repeating ideas rather than exact messages may be the best solution to avoid message fatigue. For example, the word Remain has suffered from fatigue. It was quickly converted to Remoan by the media, which further degrades the value of the term. Our populist media are experts at such things!

4. Rather than presenting features, it is better to present benefits, as some people do not translate features into benefits. A good way of forcing yourself to do this is to ask yourself the question "What does this mean for the person I'm talking with?" For example, our membership of the EU for 37 pence a week or half a Mars Bar (features) means we have had 70 + years of overall peace in Europe (benefit). This requires the use of what we call the 2nd position in Neuro-Linguistic Programming (NLP). We will return to NLP later on in this book.

Let's talk about BREX .. it

Thinking about Brexorcism

Reflect on the information above and refine your messages:

Communications model element	Applications to me
One-sided versus two sided messages Think about the intelligence level of your recipient. Is this new information or are you attempting to "over-write" an existing belief?	
Drawing conclusions When to draw it yourself? When is it best for others to draw the conclusion?	
When to repeat and when to rephrase	
Present benefits more than features Ask what the feature means for the recipient of the message?	

2. The Messenger

Successful communicators use a messenger or messengers that will be heard. I've tried many experiments where I've taken the visuals and audio away from the person delivering the message and found considerable differences in the receptivity of messages. This is especially so when the messenger is controversial in some way.

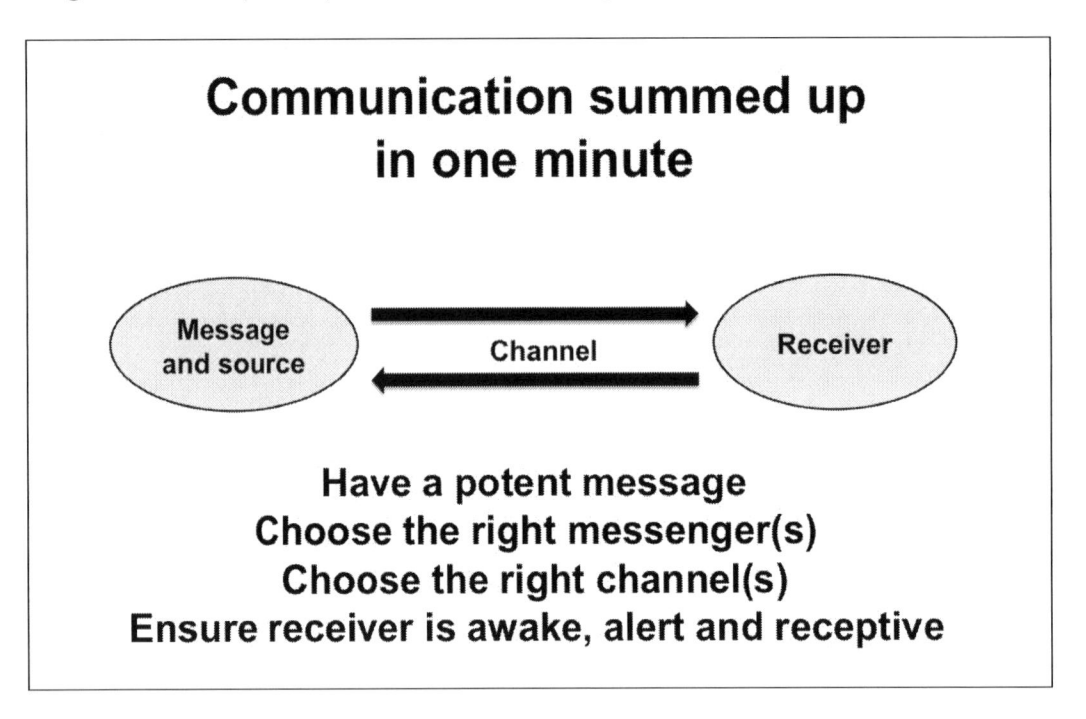

Communication summed up in one minute

Message and source ⇄ Channel ⇄ Receiver

**Have a potent message
Choose the right messenger(s)
Choose the right channel(s)
Ensure receiver is awake, alert and receptive**

I tested a speech given by ex-Prime Minister Tony Blair, talking about the need to end our Brexit process. When I simply showed the text of his speech to a group of people who did not know who had said it, their agreement with the messages was generally good. However, when I tested Blair's words matched with video and audio of him speaking on the same people, the receptivity of his message was severely impaired or fundamentally disagreed with. People offering the usual visceral reactions such as "Warmonger", "Liar", various expletives and so on. Sadly, we appear to confuse the message with the messenger. For this reason, whenever I post content by controversial figures such as Tony Blair, I usually preface the post with the title of George Michael's classic album "Listen Without Prejudice." This works quite a lot of the time, unless I am dealing with the most hardened cases.

> ## Gone Fishing
>
> I did a kind of "clinical trial" on communications with Sir Bob Geldof's famous standoff in a fishing boat on the river Thames with our UKIP fisherman Nigel Farage. Firstly, testing the message out without people knowing who said it. Then repeating with the video and audio of Bob's speech. I was surprised to note that even people who totally agreed with Geldof's message rejected it once they knew who had said it, with reactions such as "Elitist", "Rich Irish Wa...ker" and various other insults. The successful influencer chooses the right person or persons to deliver their message. This is not always themselves. So, remember that you are not always the best person to influence a particular subject.

It is particularly important to balance your innate passion for Remain with the need to persuade others of its value. Remember the point about two-sided arguments being more persuasive than one-sided ones in many circumstances. This is especially so when people believe that the messenger has something to gain from the outcome. If you find it impossible to be dispassionate and balanced about your obsession, find someone who can represent your interests in an appropriate way to your subjects.

In general, a messenger is perceived to be more influential when the receiver perceives them to be high rather than low in credibility. This explains why leaders need to operate from a strong platform of expertise to be successful. Of course, the impact of expertise is complex, since Michael Gove suggested that we need not listen to experts. Once again that goes back to the need to establish rapport before overwhelming someone with your expertise in a given subject area.

Honesty and trustworthiness are also vitally important to be an effective communicator. Therefore, the messenger's influence is weakened when the audience perceives it has something to gain from the communication. Another reason to argue on both sides of an issue when people think you are biased.

People are more easily persuaded by people they perceive to be similar to themselves. Yet the paradox for those reading this book is that we are trying to change people's minds. We may therefore be polar opposites of the people we are trying to influence. This is why it is important to find something in common with your subjects to give you some basis for conversation.

All of this information on communications and influence can be used with congruence and flair as well as an instrument of manipulation. Successful leaders know the difference and influence with integrity.

3. The Channel

Successful communicators choose the best channel(s) or media for the job at hand, not just the most convenient one(s). When we communicate, we often have a range of goals in mind, from informing, to persuading, confronting, facilitating etc. Impersonal channels can be counter-productive when giving "hard to hear" messages and this explains why people often fall out on social media channels when trying to deliver complex and emotional messages if they are any more difficult than "I love you." The relative poverty of social media as a channel for communicating nuanced messages is counterbalanced by people's shortage of time to do anything more effective. We are now in the age where deaths are announced on Facebook rather than in person, sometimes for reasons of efficiency but also with some downsides in terms of humanity.

Some examples of the poverty of communications on social media are below. These are both hilarious and rather sad at the same time:

Blaming me, Blaming EU aha

Facebook conversation about why people wanted to leave the EU – unedited.

JULIE totally agree barry . i voted leave and we won leave but getting tired of all remain voters that cant accept a simple vote decision .. if we leave and it goes to pot then so be it . but i think its all scare mongering to be honest . to fear leavers to change votes.. uk will be better out .. at least then we can concentrate on the uk citizens not saving the world problems .. no one helps our homeless our attrocities over time . my trip to france enlightened me alot of things and norway and a few other countries survive out of the EU

Let's talk about BREX .. it

Blaming me, Blaming EU aha

Facebook conversation about why people wanted to leave the EU – unedited.

JULIE Peter Cook its called financial issue plus lots of things . they say we have no money but we greatfully give away to eu . plus as in my situation i gave up my home to help people of the uk in over crowded situations . my four bed house within me leaving council moved in a two kid family just arrived in uk . i was furious and that made my mind up priority should be given to those here already needing homes . plus if you walk around the streets you will see all those that arrived to a better life in uk brought over illegally and some legal by eu law on ourstreets homeless. . i also could add even in jobs which i will add priority given to the cheap labour workers over rule our own unemployed . our produce in uk destroyed due to EU rules of size , quality etc. . . as a person who got laid off work due to cancer ,to have spent alot if time fighting for treatment , for homes for my kids , jobs not easy to get , cuts to servjces required in communities . losing everything i had ever worked for as i got cancer and had no rights to my home of 8 years . to see the nhs mess , now international health service , people fly over for treatment then go back home .i could go on but ive seen with my own eyes not media not politicians . money given to eu could be used here .. we have criminals here that cant be sent back eu laws . so so much so wrong .

i dont need to do any fact checking i have my facts and this us simply another case of remoaners bully to my facts of real life . police what do i need to report to police its full known facts to whole of uk .. i live in the real world and nothing anybody says will make me change my mind on brexit .. a uk vote won and should be followed through not all this false un factual scare mongering . other countries survive without the EU .. im not racialist either and have friends and family abroad but i care for great britain nothing more . my view is my life my families life and my grandchildrens life . honest true life situations enlighten me true facts . i also have family in politics and who work at westminster so i am aware of a little more that what media and remainers want to try tell me to be honest . nothing will make me change my mind any other way .

Quiet Reflection:

How would you answer this barrage of "stuff"?

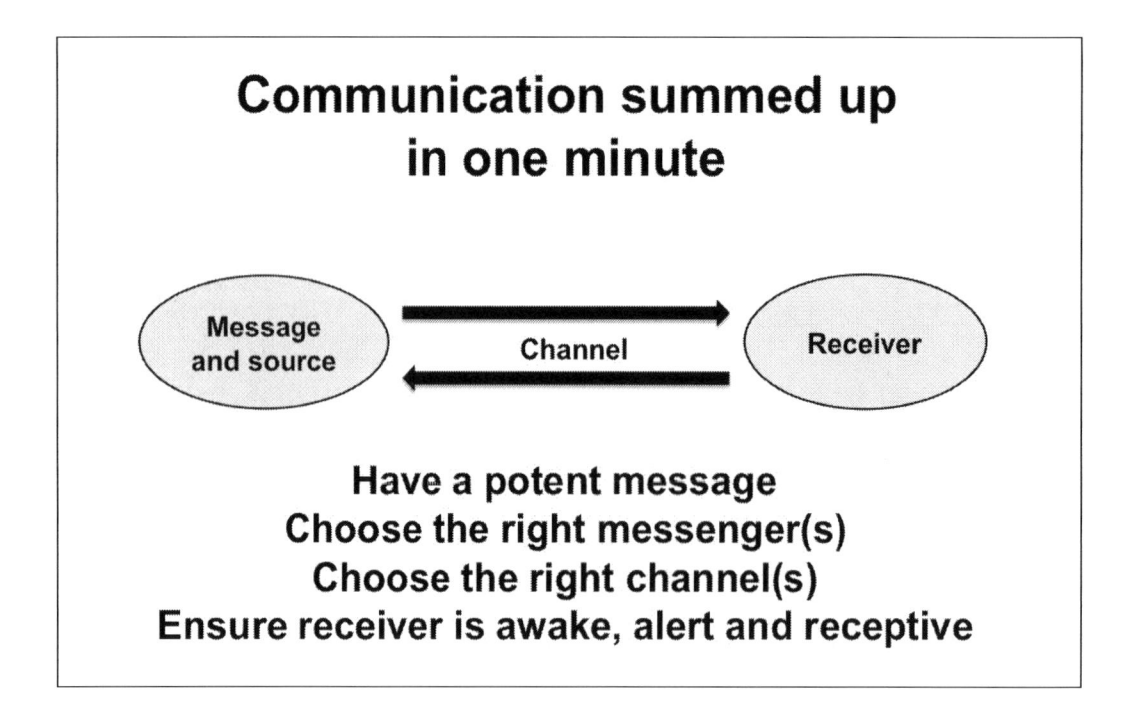

> # Communication summed up in one minute
>
> Message and source ⟷ Channel ⟷ Receiver
>
> **Have a potent message
> Choose the right messenger(s)
> Choose the right channel(s)
> Ensure receiver is awake, alert and receptive**

The multiplicity of communication channels has also increased enormously in the last 20 years from text to instant messaging across multiple platforms, video conferencing and so on, yet our fundamental skills of communicating have not changed.

Sometimes the most efficient channels are not the most effective. Personal channels such as 1:1 dialogue are expensive in terms of time but they may be very effective. Impersonal channels are much more efficient but may be quite ineffective. The successful communicator reaches for the best tool for the job rather than the one most readily available.

Two other insights from the field of NLP (Neuro-Linguistic Programming) are worthy of note here:

1. The linguistic aspects of a message are vital in terms of how effective a message is. Professor Albert Mehrabian conducted some research on personal communications in 1970 and concluded that the syntax (words), tone of voice, and body language respectively account for 7%, 38%, and 55% of personal communication. The figures are perhaps less important than the overall point, that the words chosen are but a small part of the overall communication. That said, all we have in many modern communication media (text, e-mail, messenger) is the syntax or words. This explains

why there can be so much confusion when trying to explain complex things on these media.

We regularly **delete**, **distort** and **generalise** messages through our own filters. This prompts NLP specialists to point out that "the map is not the territory." Quite literally, a map of Italy is not quite the same as the experience of visiting the country or eating a fine meal in Rome. For example, the London tube map deletes superfluous information, for example elevators, roads etc. It distorts by making the centre of London relatively bigger than outlying areas for clarity. It uses only 45 and 90-degree bends to help us to see the big picture. It also generalises information to make it easier for you to understand – colour codes for different lines, circles for interchanges etc.

What then is the relevance of deletion, distortion and generalisation in terms of giving clear, potent and accurate messages to people?

Firstly, people are fond of **deleting** context sensitive information when sending brief instant messages or texts. Simple messages do not tend to suffer from this strategy, for example "I'll meet you at the Kings Cross St Pancras Café Nero at 6.30 pm" is specific and clear. However, some people try to use the same channel to discuss matters of strategy, complexity and so on with some amusing and disastrous consequences.

Deletion of information is also quite common in my experience, when people take for granted information that you don't have access to, without which the message makes no sense at all, for example:

"He's a failure."

"A failure at what?"

Distortion of information occurs when there is an inferred cause and effect relationship, for example:

"He never brings me flowers, so he doesn't love me."

There are, of course, lots of reasons in life why flowers may not appear … not just due to an absence of love …

Communication Errors

Deletion

Missing information, either accidentally or deliberately

"Take Back Control"

Distortion

Twisted information, either accidentally or deliberately

"Turkey is joining the EU"

Generalisation

Making an all-time statement out of a specific or exception

"All immigrants are benefit scroungers"

Generalisation is an interesting area. This is the tendency of people to assume that what happens to them is true of all people. Words like all, everyone, never, always contain the hallmarks of a generalisation. Jacob Rees-Mogg and Tim Wetherspoon are fond of generalising specifics to make sweeping statements about Brexit. Spot the language patterns here:

> *"Because a sweet shop in my town is coping with Brexit transition, it means that Brexit will be plain sailing for all shop owners, towns and the country."*

> *"My pubs are booming so the whole of British industry will be fine after Brexit."*

4. The Receiver

Successful communicators ensure that those they are communicating with i.e. the receiver(s) are awake, alert and receptive. Sometimes this is the most important work you can do, to prepare people to hear what you have to say. Timing can be a crucial determinant of success. Hard to hear ideas may need some "warm-up" to get the receiver in the mood to receive. Sometimes a skilled communicator will use several staged attempts to build up interest and desire to hear what is to be said. Many of the more successful Brexorcisms I've seen and conducted are the result of a multi-stage approach with considerable warm-up and relationship building prior to any challenge.

Timing and location are also crucial if you are to reach your intended receiver and have the desired outcome. It is what I call the "Martini" effect after the retro advertisement – **not** anytime, anywhere. More like the right time, the right place etc. The successful influencer chooses the right time and the right place to make change happen.

Let's talk about BREX .. it

Thinking about Brexorcism

Reflect on the communications model and plan your interventions with key subjects:

Communications model element	Applications to me
Have a potent message How can I ensure my message is personalised? How do I ensure I respond to the other person's needs and expectations?	
Choose the right messenger(s) If the messenger(s) is not you, how can you coach the relevant person(s)?	
Choose the right communications channel(s) Remember that influence is mostly a face to face activity. If you are doing this on social media take note of the 7/38/55 factor.	
Ensure receiver(s) are awake, alert and receptive? How can I activate people to listen? How can I increase the odds that they will receive the message?	

Let's talk about BREX .. it

If you are wishing to communicate to influence and know your receivers, it is also worth considering some general personality traits that can help or hinder your cause.

- People who have low self-esteem tend to be more persuadable than someone with high self-esteem. This explains why people in distress will often take any advice even if it is inconsistent with their needs. It possibly explains why some people were willing to listen to Nigel Farage as he was supportive of the little people and boosted their self-esteem by telling them to vote with their hearts. The Remain campaign presented graphs and spreadsheets. They insisted that these same people did not understand. Whilst this may well be true, this simple presentation issue lost them votes. Worse still, it is a strategy that Remain has gold-plated to some extent ever since.

- Authoritarian personalities who are concerned about power and status are more influenced by messages from authority figures whereas non-authoritarian types are more susceptible to messages from anonymous sources. There are important implications here for the so called "metropolitan elites."

- Those high in anxiety are hard to persuade. If you face an anxious person in a difficult communications encounter, your first job is to remove their anxiety. In many 1:1 situations with Brexiteers, it is fair to say that some feel like they will be made to look stupid by speaking with you. I have made this mistake on some occasions and it is a very easy trap to fall into.

- People who are high in rich imagery, fantasies, and dreams tend to be more empathetic towards others and are more persuadable. In plain language this explains why sales people often like being sold to! Unicorn salespeople find it easy to sell unicorns to people who believe in unicorns!!

- People of high general intelligence are more influenced by messages based on impressive logical arguments and are less likely to be influenced by messages with false, illogical, or irrelevant arguments. They may be especially sensitive to short messages that appear to be unsubstantiated in our 280-character world of Twitter soundbites. There are important implications for short versus long messages here.

Let's talk about BREX .. it

Thinking about Brexorcism

Reflect on the above choices and make your own notes about your strategies for working more effectively with your target subjects:

Personality traits	Applications to me
People who have low self-esteem tend to be more persuadable than someone with high self-esteem.	
Authoritarian personalities are more influenced by messages from authority figures. Non-authoritarian types are more susceptible to messages from anonymous sources.	
Those high in anxiety are hard to persuade. Remove anxiety to be more persuasive.	
People who are high in rich imagery, fantasies, and dreams tend to be more empathetic towards others and are more persuadable.	
People of high general intelligence are more influenced by messages based on logic.	

Of course, generalisations can be generally unhelpful. It is always wise to work with the specific realities of each situation, perhaps holding this knowledge as a set of heuristics or rules of thumb rather than absolute truths.

Summary

- To communicate in order to persuade: Have a clear, potent message; use the right messenger; use the correct communications channel and; ensure the receivers are awake, alert and receptive.

- Ensuring your subject is ready to receive is the most important work you can do. If they are not listening, all your work is wasted.

- Some of the people we deal with present a barrage of issues mixed up in a ball of confusion. Alongside the skills of clear communication, we also need calmness, patience and forensic skills to help them unpick their "story" and separate general angst out from things that are related to our membership of the European Union.

- Studies of persuasive communications and personality teach us that there are certain things we can do to increase our influence in any situation. It is always good to be able to see things from your subject's viewpoint, even if you don't agree with them.

- Clear communications suffer from three basic problems: **Deletion**, **Distortion** and **Generalisation**. We will come on to some remedies for these conditions in subsequent chapters.

Chapter III
Defence Against the Dark Brexit Arts

In this chapter we drop down from the strategic heights to street level. We examine strategies to help you win friends and influence people in the great "Brexorcism" exercise that needs to take place to alter the "will of the people."

I have spent thousands of hours in cafés, bars, on the street etc. doing what J.K. Rowling would call "Defence Against the Dark Brexit Arts." I've combined some 25 years of business consulting, which is all about influence and persuasion with mastery in the psychological discipline known as NLP (Neuro-Linguistic Programming). Alongside this I have the advantage of a masters' degree in the "University of Life", gained working around the world as a business trouble-shooter and with hardened musicians in rock bands. Musicians are artistic by definition. Some are autistic. Some just p...ss artists. Musicians offer a great laboratory for practising skills of getting things done with difficult and diffident people.

I cannot possibly deliver a full tutorial in the skills needed to convert even semi-hardened leave voters in one chapter. These are skills that need hours of experiential learning through deliberate practice rather than just knowing what to do. Nonetheless I can provide the key principles and stories that illustrate these principles in practice. With practice, your skills will mature rapidly. This is really an experiential art.

You are welcome to contact me for the purposes of direct coaching, mentoring or group events in the gentle and sometimes abrasive change of changing hearts, minds and souls.

Before we begin, I'd like to offer you eleven operating assumptions that will help you be the best you can be in this area:

Defence Against the Dark Brexit Arts

Operating Assumptions

1. We do not operate directly on the world. We create 'internal maps' from our sensory experiences (sight, sounds etc.) and operate from these maps. However, the map is not the territory. Part of the job of a good change agent is to understand the operating maps of your Brexit loving clients / victims / targets, from now on known as subjects ☺
2. Choice is always better than no choice. Always seek to widen the notion of choice. We have been conditioned into binary choices with "Deal – No Deal", In – Out, British - Foreign etc.
3. If you do what you've always done, you'll get what you've always got, so if what you're doing isn't working, do something else! Flexibility is key.
4. There is no failure, only feedback, no mistakes only results, no errors, only learning. If you don't succeed in a Brexorcism, learn from it and move on.
5. Experience in itself has no meaning - all meaning is context related. When a Brexiteer tells you to get over it, it may just be a reflection of their own frustrations and anxieties. We live in a fully stressed society.
6. You cannot not communicate - 93% of communication is non-verbal. So even breathing when speaking to Brexiteers is an intervention. Especially important when your subject is unloading nearly three years of pent up angst on you!
7. The meaning of communication is the response you get, which may be different than the one you intended. By making small talk to the youths that punched me, I had hoped not to draw them into a communication loop. Clearly this did not work!
8. There is a positive intention behind all human behaviour. The youths that punched me were trying to fulfil something positive for themselves even though it seemed less positive for me. With more time and skill, I may have helped them to find less violent ways to realise their intention. Sadly, sometimes in the thick of it, there is not time to get a flip chart out and run a focus group on attitudes to anger … ☺

> # Defence Against the Dark Brexit Arts
>
> # Operating Assumptions
>
> 9. What is possible for one person is possible for others, since all humans share the same neurology. If I can wander into a café and change minds through tea and sympathy, so can you.
> 10. Each of us has or can create the resources we need to do whatever we choose. We must become opportunity seekers as there are opportunities to change minds at every bus stop, in every bar and bedroom.
> 11. The individual with the greatest flexibility of thought and behaviour can (and generally will) control the outcome of any interaction. This is why you must be agile when talking with Brexiteers. You may have noticed how some will keep changing the subject when cornered on Brexit specifics. This allows them to control the conversation.

A key skill in personal excellence is the ability to try on new assumptions.

Imagine that each of these operating assumptions is a coat which you can wear for one day to see what differences emerge. You may be surprised at the results you achieve if you act as if these assumptions are true.

Blowing Brexit Bubbles

Some Remainers tell me that they don't like talking to people who voted to leave. I understand that. It can be like dealing with dementors in the Harry Potter sense of the word. In other words, people who suck your very life force and happiness away. Typically with catchphrases such as:

"We won two wars and we can win this one."

"I want food rationing. It will teach the young respect for their elders."

"Brexit Means Brexit. End Off."

My own sister repeatedly tells me without the slightest shred of evidence that she voted leave to "prevent Sharia law on Tonbridge high street". This is a bizarre thought which she co-locates in her mind with the rise of kebab shops on the main road. However, if we don't work outside our comfort bubbles, we achieve little that will contribute towards "moving the dial" in terms of public opinion for a People's Vote or to heal the nation after Brexit ends. We are in effect, "forever blowing bubbles", so take courage people. A little confidence and some skills are needed. Renew yourselves and begin again.

I'm aware that many families and friends now avoid conversations about Brexit in social situations. However, attitudes towards Brexit have changed if you have not dared to use the B word in polite conversation for some time, with people more willing to listen to informed dialogue in many cases.

Thinking about Brexorcism

Reflect on the 11 assumptions and make your own notes about your views

NLP assumptions	Applications to me
1. The map is not the territory.	
2. Choice is always better than no choice.	
3. If you do what you've always done, you'll get what you've always got.	
4. There is no failure, only feedback.	

Let's talk about BREX .. it

Thinking about Brexorcism

NLP assumptions	Applications to me
5. All meaning is context related.	
6. You cannot not communicate.	
7. The meaning of communication is the response you get.	
8. There is a positive intention behind all human behaviour.	
9. What is possible for one person is possible for others.	
10. Each of us has or can create the resources we need to do whatever we choose.	
11. The individual with the greatest flexibility of thought and behaviour can (and generally will) control the outcome of any interaction.	

The Brexit Psyche

Conversing with hundreds of leave voters in cafés, bars and on the street over thousands of hours reveals some general traits of what the psychological discipline NLP (Neuro-Linguistic Programming) would call "meta-programmes." These are akin to the unconscious operating programmes that inform people's thoughts, feelings and behaviours. Leave voters often, but not always, because one can never generalise, think in these kinds of dimensions:

Temporal: Their time perspective is often very short term. Today, this week, this month, possibly as far ahead as a summer holiday. But there's rarely much point talking to leave voters about Jacob Rees-Mogg's 50-year Brexit scenarios, as it frequently provokes responses such as "But I'll be dead" or even "Who is Jacob Rees Mogg?" Of course, many leavers do have children and grandchildren, which can change matters, as we discuss later.

As well as people's time horizon there is also the question of people's orientation in time – in other words, whether they look to the past, present or future as their main reference points for making judgements. Empirically it turns out from thousands of conversations that many leave voters use the past as a reference point for a "golden age" when things were good, the assumption being that now or the future cannot compare in any way, shape or form. The 1950's to the 1970's seems to be the most quoted times from leave voters when "we" were doing well. Or even longer ago as this nostalgic leave voter tweets:

> "The East Coast Main Line did work rather well under the real LNER (1923-47), complete with the setting of a speed record in 1938, which stands to this day ..."

Of course, history tends to delete some of the more challenging aspects of people's memories as they age, so typhoid, rationing, the three-day week, electricity blackouts and so on are often deleted from people's longer-term memories. The "lost paradise" input to our Brexit vote was poignantly summed up by Billy Bragg in his song "Full English Brexit" in ways that words alone cannot achieve. Check the song out. Broadly speaking "nostalgia ain't what it used to be."

Let's talk about BREX .. it

My neighbours don't drink at the local
Or have kippers for breakfast like me
The food that they eat smells disgusting
They'd rather drink coffee than tea

I cheered when our side won the Cold War
Spread freedom and peace all around
Now there's folks speaking Russian in Tesco's
It's a shame the wall had to come down

Billy Bragg – Full English Brexit www.billybragg.co.uk

Status Quo, Gammon, Chips and Beer

Tim Wetherspoon cleverly capitalises on the "lost paradise" aspect of older leave voters though his political campaigns in Wetherspoons pubs, his fine taste for old buildings, no-nonsense cheap food and beer. In fairness the pub environments are not 1970's, the staff are friendly but most other things are. I'm just surprised that "Chicken in the basket" is not on the menu. I can only assume that that damn EU banned the baskets as unhygienic!

A pub chat with the manager and staff in one of their outlets tells me that staff actually like the social atmosphere of their fellow workers, they mostly hate Tim but keep quiet and we cannot blame them for that in a gig economy that provides little in long term employment. Amazingly, they were not only happy for me to place anti Brexit stickers in the pub, they actually encouraged it.

So be nice to Wetherspoons' staff. It is not exactly their fault! Whether you love or hate him personally you cannot deny that Tim strategy is future focused for him … it seems to me that he seeks market dominance by pushing prices down to a level where independent pubs cannot compete. Once he has achieved that, he can do what he likes … except that large segments of his clientele are a dying breed … we'll see what happens with his idea of a full English Brexit food menu … I guess that will be curry then …

Spatial: In terms of geography, a leave voter's compass often centres around their house and family, their street, their town, possibly England but rarely further. I was listening into a café conversation recently, where a small group of old leavers were "celebrating the advent of blue passports." I was quietly bemused to find the café owner asking them when they last left the country. It turned out that none of them had ever travelled abroad. Three of them (from four) had never even visited London (30 miles / 49 minutes by train) in some 60 + years on planet earth. Globalisation does not mean much to such people. It is bewildering and we achieve little by discussing it apart from sounding like elitists, unless they bring it up as part of their rationale for leaving the EU, for which there are clear answers.

Self-centredness: In terms of self or other centricity, I note with some sadness that there is rarely any ability to see Brexit from any viewpoint other than their own. Human beings are basically animals and our sense of self-preservation is a primal instinct unless we actively choose to over-ride it consciously. So, appeals based on worldliness, selflessness or greater good type approaches can fall on deaf ears. We hear this played out when people say we should look after our own when they criticise charitable activity or world aid programmes. In NLP terminology, some leave voters have trouble getting into "second" position, certainly "third", where they can see things from other perspectives outside their own. At the same time these people can demonstrate remarkable detachment. In extremis this is demonstrated graphically by the likes of faux celebrity Katie Hopkins who reported:

> *"Show me bodies floating in the water, play violins and show me skinny people looking sad. I don't care."*

The F words: in a lot of cases, leave voters want to leave the EU based on **feelings** which have been carefully and consistently ingrained as hard beliefs over many years through consumption of lies from the populist media. These were reinforced in the referendum through catchy slogans by the likes of Nigel Farage. Fighting **feelings** with **facts** can be a very difficult game to play as you are confronting quasi-religious beliefs with information and this is not an equal contest for someone who has almost been radicalised. Hence my use of the term "Brexorcism" in this book. Even broadcaster James O'Brien finds it difficult to gain acceptance from his callers when he provides facts that counter their firmly felt feelings. We must recognise that change may occur after an interaction and his LBC Radio show is necessarily limited by the fact that it is mostly a time constrained and single shot theatre for conversation. But, of course, people have the opportunity to hear themselves not listening on playback which must be a painful experience for some as they experience the pain that comes from "cognitive dissonance" as they try to hold two opposing thoughts in their minds about a topic simultaneously.

Now, of course, we could rant on here about what is wrong with such people but it does no good. Seek first to gain rapport, understand their viewpoint, however dissonant it is with yours. At this point you stand a better chance of changing hearts and minds if you respond flexibly.

Neuro-Linguistic Programming offers a different take on how we think via what it calls meta language patterns:

Language Pattern	Behaviour	Brexit applications
Towards or away from	Whether people move towards pleasure or away from pain.	This neatly explains why some Brexiteers discount project fear and why others are persuaded by vague promises of better times.
External or internally referenced	The extent to which people evaluate things using their own internal filters or using external criteria.	This may partly explain why Brexiteers were persuaded to vote with their hearts by Nigel Farage and why external data was ignored.
Self or other centred-ness	The "what's in it for me" factor versus a more systemic view i.e. what they can do for themselves or others.	We have already discussed that some Brexiteers seem to have a more limited field of vision regarding the meaning of Brexit.
Sort for the familiar or difference	Familiar things are given preference than difference.	Conversations with Brexiteers suggest that some feel alienated by many things these days. Although few of these things are caused by the EU, it is a convenient coat-hanger to hang problems on.

Language Pattern	Behaviour	Brexit applications
Convincer strategy	What does it take to convince someone that something is true?	A fundamental error in the referendum campaign was the belief that if people thought they would be worse off they would vote to stay in the EU.
Possibility versus necessity	The extent that people focus on just what they need or what they want.	The leave campaign offered an opulent vision of freedom and a land of milk and honey without specifying how any of this might be deliverable.
Independent thinking versus group think	The extent to which people are independent thinkers or whether they follow the herd.	The importance of this cannot be overstated when considering broadcast media such as The Sun, Mail, Express, consumed in cafés and so on

Blank Canvases and Restoring the Brexit Mind

How then do we re-format minds that have already been "programmed" over many years? With great difficulty is a starting answer but it can be done. In the world of art, it is much easier to paint on a blank canvas than one that has already been painted on … In other words, the populist press had already etched firmly held beliefs on these people's minds over many years. Challenging such ingrained views is rather like trying to apply an aggressive paint stripper to their minds or undo a writeable CD that has already been written on and finalised. The technical term for this is unlearning. It is much harder than learning as it requires the "undo" step.

To stand a chance in this dark art, extensive preparation is required. You almost need to get permission and agreement to perform the "Brexorcism." Sometimes it helps if your subject does not even know that they are being reprogrammed. Social settings are good for this and sometimes understated methods can seep into people's minds better than the standard tools of selling and persuasion. Great influence is often an artform which is almost invisible to the recipient. This is why I sometimes wander into cafés and bars with apparently no agenda, letting my subjects or "victims" come to me, usually via an initial interaction with a T-shirt, badge or artefact. Over nearly three years of doing this I find that some of my best work is almost invisible to the untrained eye.

NLP unplugged

Neuro-Linguistic Programming (NLP) comes with a mixed reputation. It is said that NLP master Paul Mc Kenna helped Vote Leave create the snappy slogans that helped them win the referendum, as a friend of Aaron Banks. If that's not a good enough testimony to its power, then I'm not sure what is. NLP has of course been linked with ideas about mind manipulation, spin and other things which people see as negative. NLP is neutral.

The degree to which NLP is used or abused lies with the people using it. But I am aware that some find it hard to separate the tool from the person. I am going to do that here, offering you a digest of the main ideas of value to people trying to achieve change in the minds of Brexiteers. I have spent many years studying NLP and related psychologies and a casual read of this book will not make you a master of the art and discipline. But it will supplement your own experience and common sense in making better interventions.

NLP is not a theory. It is a model of what works. The test of a theory is whether it is right or wrong. The test of a model is its usefulness. Unlike other models that tell you **what** you need to do, NLP shows you **how** to do it.

There are numerous definitions of NLP - one of the most useful ones is:

NLP is the study of the effect of language, both verbal and non-verbal in producing excellence in human communications, to achieve desired results.

The awkward name comes from the developments of cognitive science in the 1970's, when research into the brain and the nervous system began to overlap with artificial intelligence studies in the computer field, producing enormous leaps in our understanding of the 'mind'. Although Neuro-Linguistic Programming is a pretty long title, the separate terms precisely identify its meaning:

Neuro About your brain and its function

Linguistic How language affects the way you see the world, both syntax (the words) and body language

Programming About our ability to make different choices in life

NLP offers us a simple and flexible formula for influential communications to get things done. In a nutshell:

NLP in a nutshell

To achieve anything in life, you need to do four things:

1. Gain **rapport** with the person(s) you wish to influence.

2. Know what you want with precision. This is your **outcome**.

3. Notice responses of others, verbal and non-verbal. This is **acuity**.

4. Keep changing what you do until you get the outcomes you want. This is **flexibility**.

Other ways of saying this include:

If you always do what you always did, you'll always get what you always got. So, if what you're doing isn't working, do something else!

… or, more cynically if you are that way inclined:

One definition of insanity is doing the same things and expecting a different result!

The formula is easy to write down, but not in common use!!

NLP provides practical tools and underpinning values for achieving each part of the formula. Taking these in turn:

1. Gaining rapport

It is impossible to influence anyone if you do not have bond of trust, even if this is limited to the terms of the current interaction that you are involved with. Rapport usually arises naturally when two people share something in common. Obviously when working with leavers you are working with people which you have difference built in by design. So, we must look in other places to find a common bond. This can of course be a myriad of things – music, football, fitness, hobbies and so on

Where there are no natural sources of rapport but you still need to make progress in an interaction, the idea of **matching** the other person's observable behaviour, e.g. language, voice tone and quality, body language etc. may give some basic rapport.

Conversely when you wish to disconnect from a conversation or change the subject, try **mismatching**. This can be subtle and we do it all the time by looking at our watch, using gestures and so on, but it can be done deliberately without causing offence.

Once you have rapport, focus on your outcome for the interaction.

2. Know your outcome

Well-formed **outcomes** are ones that drive success in an interaction. For example, do you really need your Brexiteers to become enthusiastic advocates for Remaining in the EU or is it merely sufficient to take them to a point of indifference towards the EU from the point of view of a People's Vote? The tactics to achieve the former are much harder than the latter. Too many Remainers seek a full 180-degree religious conversion to Remain when a move to what business gurus call a "zone of indifference" or a 90-degree refocus (no longer wish to Brexit or complete indifference to voting again) may be sufficient for a pragmatic approach.

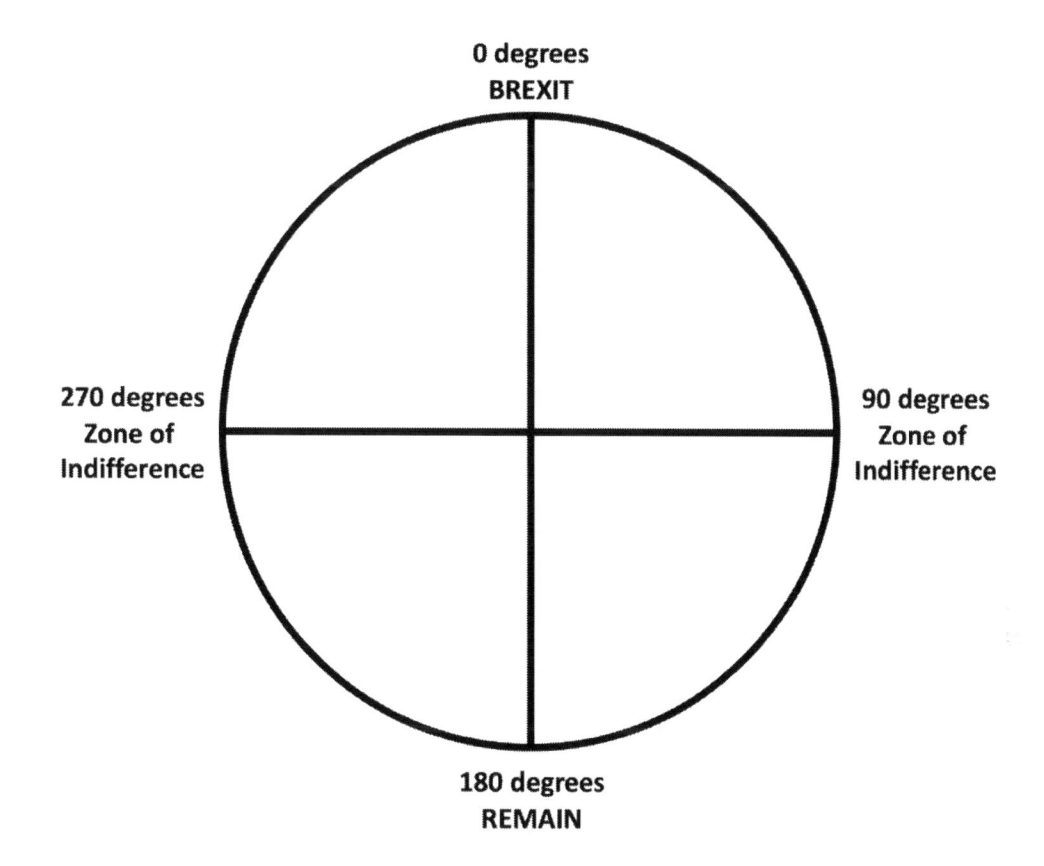

```
                    0 degrees
                     BREXIT

  270 degrees                         90 degrees
   Zone of                              Zone of
 Indifference                        Indifference

                    180 degrees
                      REMAIN
```

NLP offers specific tools to help you clarify goals and outcomes which are outside the scope of this book. Outcomes are often shared in the world of business as it is essential for others to share in the goal. In the case of influencing a leave voter there are occasions when the goal will be shared, for example in a panel debate or radio interview when the other person will know that you are taking an opposing view. In other cases, you may be working underground. Machiavelli would advise that you can only have a conspiracy of one person!

3. Acuity

"Seek first to understand."

Acuity is a fancy word for using **all** of your senses for the purpose of listening, rather than just using your ears. It has been shown that body language represents 55% of any interpersonal communication message, voice tone 38% and the words only 7%. This helps to explain the myriad of misunderstandings that occur on social media when you really only have the 7% of communication plus a few emoticons in your toolkit. In the case of Brexit, we are often trying to explain quite complex concepts using less than 280 characters on Twitter to people that may well be on a completely different wavelength, so there is no basic rapport or shared outcome. I'm not saying that dialogue on social media is pointless as a tool of influence, but it is important to be aware of the limitations compared with face to face communications.

Listening is thus an active process, going beyond the actual words used. Furthermore, different people use different senses to make sense of what is happening, i.e. sight, sound, feelings, taste and smell. These thinking styles "leak out in our language", e.g. I can **see** what you mean, and I **feel** that it will work out. One can of course match the language of your subject to make them feel like you understand them better.

4. Flexibility of thought and deed

"If you have no choice you are dead
If you have one choice, you have no choice
If you have two choices, you have a dilemma
If you have three or more choices, you have the makings of a real choice"

The more points of view you have, the better off you are with respect to being influential. Flexibility of thought **and** behaviour are required if you want to get a different response in a given situation.

Human beings communicate in a **system**. In other words, if one party varies their response, the other side has to respond differently, provided they are listening to you. This is flexibility of **behaviour**. So, if your subject is saying we must take back control, break the pattern by asking what part of control matters to him or her:

Flexibility of **thinking** arises if you change your perception of a situation. Expert influencers know that, in any situation of interpersonal influence, there are at least three points of view:

1. Your own   Known as 1st position in NLP

2. The other person's   Known as 2nd position in NLP

3. The viewpoint of a "detached" observer   Known as 3rd position in NLP

On flexibility

If you always do what you always did, you will always get what you always got ...

So, if what you are doing isn't working, do something different ...

Use 1ˢᵗ, 2ⁿᵈ, 3ʳᵈ position

If you are not getting enough of what you want in a situation, try altering the "position" from which you are operating, notice what is different and then modify your behaviour accordingly. Practical manifestations of this include asking your subject to switch positions. Innocent questions are the breakfast of champions in this area, for example:

"You have told me you want your country back. Where did it go? Who took it? When did it leave?"

"How do you know it was taken? What has been lost?"

"What specifically do you want back?"

"What do your children think about this?"

Thinking about Brexorcism

NLP process	Applications to me
Gaining **rapport**	
Know your **outcome**	
Have **acuity** – open all the senses	
Practice **flexibility**	

Let's talk about BREX .. it

On flexibility

My sources tell me that Remain is in danger of copying the design that lost them the referendum ... hiring the same faces with the same strategies that did not perform well in 2016.

Nigel Farage et al. had clear strategies, the advantage of a pliable followers etc. But it is never a good idea to copy someone's strategy. That just takes you to a point of equivalence.

If you can't beat them, better them

How can you be more flexible to achieve more?

Enter the Dementor

To be an effective influencer, try finding things you can agree on with your leave voter. They need not be lies however if you are to retain your sense of integrity. In Harry Potter terms it is what I call "Entering the Dementor." It is what NLP refers to as "pacing and leading." Pacing is when you are in the other person's reality, in their shoes so to speak. Leading is when you are operating from your own point of view and literally leading them to see different realities. A story serves to illustrate the principle:

Trumptown and Brexit

I was talking to a pub owner on The Isle of Sheppey. He had fought for his country in the Falklands, came back to the UK and felt let down by the UK. This is a familiar story. I have seen it when wandering around military fairs and talking to veterans and "Help for Heroes" supporters. It is not without some justification. Many people joined the army expecting a cradle to grave care package. It is now largely left to the third sector to provide support for injured forces personnel.

His pub was empty. Another source of angst, although not one that was caused by the EU. He told me he wanted to leave the UK with his Russian wife to live in the US as a committed Brexit and Trump supporter. He was not expecting me to agree that he was right to feel fed up.

Once we had established that (pacing), he found it a bit easier to hear the point that, whilst he was right to feel fed up and left behind, he was wrong to blame the EU for his regrets. I had separated the effect (angst) from the cause. I was helped significantly by the fact that he really hated the Corbynista "Billy Bragg" protester who also frequented the pub. He told me "at least you can fu..king sing and play" … faint praise … He also hated Corbyn and the proselytization of the other performer about a return to Communism in Britain … The lesson learned here is that we must take rapport from wherever it comes!

I had given him credit for some of his analysis, giving me a small "bank balance" to draw on in order to challenge him about the source of his concerns.

Let's talk about BREX .. it

> ## Trumptown and Brexit
>
> In truth it took a little time to get him to listen (I did not achieve it in one single session and incubation time is often helpful). I had "warmed him up" over a few months through musical performances. This included getting him to participate with a performance of our Chas & Dave Cockney Brexit Knees Up "Boll..cks to Brexit" (See www.brexitrage.com) beforehand. Finding ways to loosen up your "client" is all part of the skill of a change agent. It is what Kurt Lewin discussed when he used the terms unfreezing, changing and refreezing. Unfreezing your victim does not have to involve making them do a "Chas & Dave Cockney Brexit Knees Up" however! It can be as simple as spending time listening to them, buying them a drink and so on.

Summary

- Great communicators systematically create rapport with people they have little in common with.
- They are clear on their outcome for an intervention or series of interventions. This may merely mean gaining acceptance for an alternative viewpoint or a complete 180-degree Brexorcism.
- They pay good attention to their subject through acuity and respect their viewpoints, regardless of their legitimacy or accuracy.
- Crucially they maintain flexibility. This means shifting shapes in response to the other person's response rather than holding onto positions and ideologies.
- A key skill is that of **pacing** (being in the subject's position and viewpoint) and **leading** when appropriate. This involves the use of what NLP calls 1st, 2nd and 3rd position.
- The use of 1st, 2nd and 3rd position also gives you the possibility of being more influential than your subject. Do it with empathy to avoid seeming arrogant.
- Context is everything and successful influencers warm their subjects up for a Brexorcism, sometimes over time.

Chapter IV
It ain't what you do, it's the way that you do it: Communication styles

Great communicators adopt a range of styles that are consistent with the Brexorcism outcome they seek. They systematically work through the flexible process for changing minds that we described in the last chapter:

- Gaining **rapport** with their subject(s).
- Setting clear **outcomes** for an intervention or series of interventions.
- Paying attention to their subject through **acuity** and respect for their viewpoints regardless of their legitimacy.
- Acting with **flexibility**. This means shifting shapes in response to the other person's response.

Skilled communicators use the entire spectrum of behavioural styles available to them. Sometimes they use "push" approaches. At other times they "pull".

In this chapter we consider the full range of styles of interpersonal communications' styles available to you. I find John Heron's model of intervention styles especially relevant, since these cover interventions across the spectrum from **directive** to **non-directive**. Heron's model was originally developed for therapeutic interventions. It is therefore very applicable to the act of "Brexorcism", since we are often working at the level of fundamental beliefs change, even identity in some cases. The model flags up the many roles that a great Brexorcist must be willing and able to use.

Heron's model covers six styles, broken into two types:

Directive, where you are overall in control of the interaction, and;

Non-Directive, which offers your subject shared control of the interaction.

Direction is usually a quicker. However, non-directive approaches offer a greater possibility of ownership of any changes that are achieved by the person you are trying to influence. In practice master communicators move between these modes with flair.

To observe this in practice, tune into James O'Brien on LBC. His radio show operates under a necessary constraint of time and of course O'Brien is a broadcaster, so he tends to use more of the directive approaches. However, on occasion, you will hear him using the most delightful catalytic and cathartic approaches, even supporting styles when he says things like:

"Look, you are a good man and I don't want to fall out with you over this."

Here are the six styles, broken into the two modes of interaction: **Directive** and; **Non-Directive**. These broadly correspond with "push" and "pull", although they are a little subtler than this binary division implies:

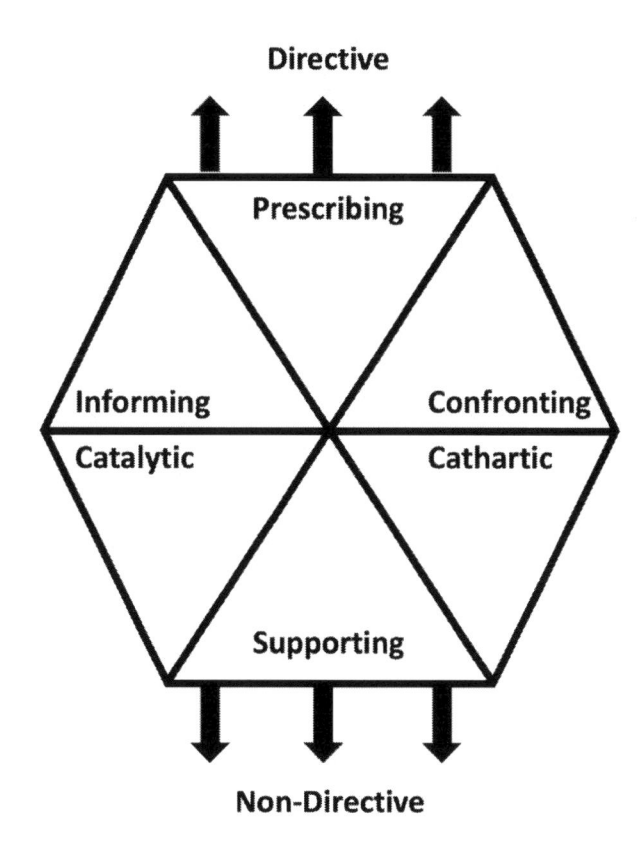

Directive

Prescribing

Informing | Confronting
Catalytic | Cathartic

Supporting

Non-Directive

The NLP Process

Rapport

Without rapport you ain't got nothin'

Outcome

Stick to your outcome, not your position

Acuity

Open all your orifices to receive

Flexibility

The most flexible person will generally control the outcome

Prescribing (Directive): Essentially a "tell" style. For example:

"Take these pills and you'll feel better."

Prescribing is probably the quickest way to get someone to do something. However, the quickest way is not always the most effective way. We know full well that we don't always take the doctor's advice if it does not accord with our own wants, whims and fancies as articulated by the Dunning-Kruger effect, where people of low ability tend to assess their own cognitive abilities as being superior to experts and vice versa. It is perhaps for this reason that the other styles exist, since we are not that great at taking direct advice if it is dissonant with our prevailing paradigm.

Informing (Directive): Neutrally passing on information, ideas and knowledge. For example:

"I can tell you that Remain now have a 16-point lead in the polls."

This gives your subject the chance to make their own minds up without feeling pressurised or manipulated. Informing does not draw a conclusion. It simply provides neutral information, leaving the recipient to draw their own conclusions and formulate actions. However, one then needs a lot of time for your subject to process the information provided to them and come up with options and actions to address the need. There is of course always a risk that the information will be processed but no action will result or possibly the "wrong" course of action. Whilst informing may be more effective in the long-term, it requires more time and processing power than prescribing.

Confronting (Directive): Involves challenging viewpoints and requires the examination of motives. For example:

"You said that you are not a racist, but you keep saying that you hate people from Eastern Europe. I'm finding it hard to understand what you are saying"

Confronting should not be confused with aggression – it can be done with a soft pillow as well as a hard edge. Confronting is however one of the more difficult interventions that you can undertake as it usually results in some level of cognitive dissonance, where people are held to account or get "found out". Done with skill, it can be very effective and relatively quick, but once again the Dunning-Kruger effect applies and people can become actively defensive or, worse still, passively so, which is harder to spot.

Non-directive interventions usually take longer than directive ones. After all they are literally less "direct". However, they may be very effective in more troublesome situations. They also require greater levels of skill and sleight of hand techniques to make them work. The TV detective Columbo is a great place to study these interventions used in a particular direction. Columbo rarely confronts his suspects, using a series of much more subtle but clever interventions to smoke the culprits out. Far from a simple piece of entertainment, I discovered from the Metropolitan Police Diplomatic Protection Group that they use Columbo at Hendon Police College to train their top detectives for similar reasons that I've described here, contrasting the approach with some less-effective approaches from other TV copumentaries.

Cathartic (Non-Directive): Interventions that enable people to "get things off their chest." For example:

> *"Can we spend some time exploring why freedom of movement only applies to EU Citizens coming to UK but not to Brits wishing to travel abroad?"*

Catharsis can be extremely powerful as a means of allowing people to relive tension about things that are hard to express in more direct terms. One example of this is the use of extended metaphor, where you ask your subject to describe the issue under discussion in metaphorical terms. Sometimes this level of detachment allows people to say hard to say or unsayable things. See also our discussion on 2nd and 3rd position from NLP earlier.

Catalytic (Non-Directive): Providing a sounding board and helping others to come up with their own solutions. For example:

> *"Would you like to explain more about what Brexit will offer you personally?"*

Catalytic interventions build on the idea of catalysis in chemistry. A catalyst is used in small doses to promote a reaction but is itself not involved in the actual reaction and remains unchanged at the end of that reaction. It is once again a detached position to take for the influencer, giving your subjects space to reflect, consider novel ideas and rethink old approaches.

Supporting (Non-Directive): Feedback to your subject in which they are actively listened to and encouraged in what they are doing. For example:

> *"I can understand why you would feel left behind."*

Let's talk about BREX .. it

Supporting is often of great value when using the more challenging interventions in Heron's model. It provides the essential positive assets in the "bank balance" between you and your subject to draw on when dealing with more challenging elements. In general it is always wise to use plenty of pull strategies if you are also pushing for change and a sensible ratio is at least 2:1 pull:push. It is also important to consider the "rhythm" of your interventions. After all, change is like a dance at some level and keeping in step with those you are attempting to engage in the dance of change is important if you are to maintain a high conversion ratio of thoughts into actions.

Great influencers are both well-prepared and also great improvisers to follow lines of enquiry, balancing the need for direction with the need to induce thinking and action within their subjects.

Heron's model can be taken to new levels when you consider the possibility as to whether you have authority in an interaction. If you do, it may be possible to act as if you are in a hierarchy. More normally in a conversation with a Brexit voter, we are on a level playing field, even if we think we are smarter than they are. This requires that we move towards the right-hand side of the grid, from co-operation through to giving the person full autonomy.

Some examples illustrate the point well:

I often suggest that Brexiteers fact check their own information biases as, of course, they naturally assume I am myself biased! In society we often operate without any hierarchy and it is not usually feasible to try to pull rank on people you meet casually in cafés, on streets and so on. If the person I meet appears to lack the skills needed to help themselves, I will often help them, for example, by asking them to:

1. Get their phone out.
2. Get on Google.
3. Type in the question or issue that is troubling them.

By operating in co-operative mode and allowing them to use their own phone, it gives greater sense of ownership, even though this usually takes longer.

Let's talk about BREX .. it

Six Styles of Brexorcism

Prescribing

A tell style.

Informing

Neutral supply of information without judgement.

Confronting

Holding the mirror up to your subject.

Cathartic

Helping your subject unload.

Catalytic

Stimulating new thinking with minimal provocation.

Supporting

Giving credit where it is due.

Let's talk about BREX .. it

Thinking about Brexorcism

Reflect on the six intervention styles and consider which ones are your strongest skills Plan to develop the others through deliberate practice outside your current comfort levels. Consider where they will be of benefit:

Intervention style	Strength / development areas and potential benefits
Prescribing (Directive)	
Informing (Directive)	
Confronting (Directive)	
Cathartic (Non-Directive)	
Catalytic (Non-Directive)	
Supporting (Non-Directive)	

Let's talk about BREX .. it

James O'Brien qualifies for expert status. In theory, he could therefore use hierarchical mode on his LBC radio show, you will often hear him practising what I call "naïve listening" in order to promote self-enquiry on the part of his callers. This is especially skilled given the time pressure he is under to deliver entertaining radio without long pauses as his callers re-arrange their synapses to sort out the cognitive dissonance that arises!

I have developed the model below to show how you can operate in the various modes, from hierarchical to autonomous:

	Style	Hierarchical	Co-operative	Autonomous
D I R E C T I V E	**Prescribing**	It would in your best interests to read up about the 270 Irish border crossings.	Let's look at some websites so that we can both understand the Irish border question.	What about calling the Irish embassy to find out some information first hand.
	Informing	Look at your Council Tax bill. The EU costs around 2.0% of your tax. The total for the NHS and social care is 48%	Let's have a look at our Council Tax bills to see where our money goes.	I have some information which I would like you to consider. Let me know how you would like to move forward?
	Confronting	You told me 7 times that we must take back control of our laws. However, you cannot name a single law which affects you.	I am concerned that we don't appear to be able to resolve the dilemma about which EU laws trouble you. Let's look at these one by one together?	Please call this person. He is a respected EU lawyer and will be able to tell you which laws are made by the EU and which by our own Government.

Let's talk about BREX .. it

	Style	Hierarchical	Co-operative	Autonomous
N O N D I R E C T I V E	Cathartic	Now is a good time for you to tell me what you really think about immigration.	Can we spend some time exploring what it feels like for someone who came to this country 20 years ago and who now feels like they don't belong here?	Would you like to tell me how you feel about the immigrants in your town and your own experience of interacting with them?
	Catalytic	Explain to me what you think you have learned about Brexit since the day we voted.	Let's explore the differences between what was promised in the Brexit "brochure" and what has come to pass.	Would you like to come back to me to explain what Brexit has come to mean to you now?
	Supporting	I think you made the right decision when you voted, given our knowledge on both sides at that time.	I sense that you are having difficulty talking about your disappointments over Brexit. Perhaps we can explore how we both feel now.	I'll support you whatever it is you finally decide about voting in a 2nd referendum Brexit.

If you are fortunate to develop long term relationships with Brexiteers over time, it is sometimes possible to get elevated to hierarchical mode. But you must earn your right to be an expert in a social situation. The café example below shows how a long-term approach using non-directive conversation using catalytic, cathartic and supportive styles can get you "promoted" and your expertise validated. Once this happens, people will both listen to you about Brexit and may even solicit your opinion on the topic. Once that happens, you stand a much greater chance of achieving Brexorcism.

Café Catalysis

The slow percolation of change is often more effective than a single "espresso" shot. I have been going to a local café in my area over an extended period. The café owner always talks to me about my anti-Brexit activities. We always keep it light and amusing. Most importantly, I never talk about politics to her regular customers (all leave voters, 60 + years old). However, I know they listen in to our conversations. Over time they became curious about what I did. They began by asking the café owner if I was a politician (after I'd left of course … it is not English to ask the person!)

After some months the café owner told me that they had searched and found me on Facebook. It turned out that they knew more about my daily movements than I do on occasions! The enigma of my activities on Downing Street was amplified by my taking my bicycle in the café with my "Break Brexit Before Brexit Breaks Britain" signage, my "F...CK Brexit" T-Shirt and so on. I always talk to the café owner about current developments on Brexit but made a rule never to proselytise to her customers about Brexit. I know they listen in. When I speak with them it is simply to join in with the general conversation of the day. I would of course listen in to their conversations about having to queue for the doctors due to immigrants and all the usual stuff, nodding sufficiently and acknowledging their frustrations to gain rapport without actually agreeing with them.

A tipping point occurred when I got punched for my T-Shirt. I did not mention it but found out from the café owner that they had already found out from Facebook. On my next visit to the café, resplendent with two black eyes, they started asking me about whether I was going to prosecute and so on. They were surprised that I shrugged my shoulders and just said that we cannot let one incident rule our lives. I did not lecture them about the fact that Brexit had legitimised and even encouraged this behaviour as they were so shocked about it. I thought it better to let them draw their own conclusions in what Heron calls "autonomous" mode. Shrugging is sometimes a more useful strategy than lecturing! All things in their place.

Let's talk about BREX .. it

> ## Café Catalysis
>
> Over time and by not intervening, they now ask me questions about Brexit and are gradually forming the view that Brexit is a mess regardless of what they voted for. My extreme non-directive behaviour over time has paid dividends, but it has also cost me a lot in Earl Grey Tea, sympathy and patience!
>
> - Where are your opportunities for a drip feed approach?
> - Where and when can you be more laid back in order to promote more autonomous or co-operative approaches to self-induced Brexorcism?
> - What subtle (or otherwise) signs and symbols can you use to help start difficult conversations about Brexit?
> - Do you think that Earl Grey is essential for success? Would Yorkshire Tea or coffee work just as well?

Reversing family hierarchies

I am the last in a line of 6 children with some 27 years between all the siblings. My mother lost her first husband in World War II and started over. It is generally acknowledged that I'm probably the brightest of the family but that cuts no ice over family hierarchy through age. My sister in particular adopts a matriarchal approach and I'm still very much considered subordinate in most respects. This has not caused us any problems throughout our lives but it came to a head after Brexit.

At Sunday Tea one afternoon, shortly after the Brexit referendum, my sister and her husband revealed that they voted leave and an argument broke out. Incidentally, it turned out that their own children also had heated words with them. One has a German wife. The other feared for his job as he and his children work in financial services.

My sister admits that she does not understand much about politics and current affairs. So, when it was time to vote, her decision was influenced by what she saw as informed sources i.e. The Daily Mail / Express. Her main argument for leaving the EU was because she did not want Sharia Law on Tonbridge High Street. Her husband cited the spectre of some two million Turkish rapists coming to Britain from Berlin.

A heated argument broke out which I was not able to win, despite being in possession of more accurate information. Remember, this was early after the referendum and I had not realised just how deeply seated these myths and legends had been installed via our media. Eventually I went to the kitchen to make tea and decided I could face no more. I left my own house and returned once they had gone home.

The point here is that my expertise in the situation was not accepted as a valid part of our transaction. The operating theory in my family is that age is more important than knowledge. You may well ask what I have done about this since to reverse this family hierarchy? Well, I wrote a letter to my sister and her husband explaining in detail how I had found the whole matter extremely hurtful and that I no longer wished to see them. This clearly hurt my sister who did have the courtesy to reply.

We have not yet reached the point where her husband is willing to acknowledge that his illusion about the two million Turkish rapists was a lie. I don't need him to do this really. I do however need them to say that they would vote differently if a People's Vote were called.

So, beware of the trap of acting as if you are in a hierarchy if there is no agreement about that within a particular social setting. Expertise and authority must be earned as with our previous example of "Café Catalysis".

Politicians also make the mistake of assumed hierarchy. In their case, they assume that, because they have been elected, they have authority by dint of their position in society. Western society does not always respect position power these days. Just think. When some people get a diagnosis of illness by a doctor these days, they sometimes challenge the doctor or seek a second opinion.

The 3R's of Brexorcism:

Rewind

Reload

Reprogram

Some subjects just want to tell you their life story. There can be a profound benefit in just rewinding their life without doing anything other than listening and maybe making the odd non-directive intervention. The rapport that you may generate from this may allow you to separate their story from feelings that the EU are responsible for their story. In a sense, you can allow them to reload their story.

In other cases, re-programming may be needed. A complete reboot, challenging beliefs and identity level change. One useful rule of thumb here is that people have to change a behaviour something like 20 times for it to become embedded as a new habit. Changing viewpoints on Brexit may therefore be something like the change needed to deal with addictions.

Summary

- Knowing what to do in a Brexorcism is one thing. Knowing how to do it is quite another. Your style of intervention may well determine how well your message is received.

- We often think of influence as a sales process and, indeed, it is in part. However, when we are trying to change beliefs, push marketing approaches can be less effective.

- Some of the strategies which we call non-directive can be very effective in helping people rewind, reload and re-program themselves.

- Some of the most effective changes are self-induced. A good facilitator knows.

- Personalisation is key. People notice authenticity and that often comes from your own personal experience. Check out our Top Tips for Defence Against the Dark Brexit Arts.

Top Tips for Defence Against the Dark Brexit Arts

Play to your strengths: If you are great at push approaches and not so good at the pull ones, plan to develop the latter whilst finding ways to minimise any weaknesses. Perhaps that means working in tandem with someone who is good at the things you are less good at (Tag Brexorcism) or choosing subjects that are more amenable to push style influence.

Know your outcome: Are you planning a 90 or 180-degree Brexorcism? Is it feasible to do this in the allotted time? Be realistic in setting goals for change.

Maintain flexibility: Stick to your outcome rather than your position. If what you are doing is not working, do something different.

Keep focus: Many Brexiteers, when confronted, change the subject. Politely but firmly maintain focus e.g. "You said you wanted to talk about immigration but we are now talking about garlic. Can we return to the subject when you are ready?"

Preparation is key: Don't rush headlong into a Brexorcism until all the preliminaries have been dealt with. Seemingly trivial things matter such as small talk, getting the environment conducive to good listening and so on.

Make it personal: Tell your own story if people want to listen. Stories seep into people's hearts and often bypass their heads. Listen to Nigel Farage if you are not convinced. The technical term for this is "self-disclosure". Telling someone that you are worried or frightened can be a powerful lever, especially if it runs counter-culture to expected societal norms. For example, a man telling another man he is fearful for his family may be counter cultural in some settings.

Chapter V
Mind your language

Neuro-Linguistic Programming (NLP) has a whole section on linguistics and there is far too much to go into here, having spent some five years learning from masters of their art and discipline, but I will provide an essential digest here ... suffice to say that the language you use has a huge impact on how another person will perceive you and ultimately how influential your message will be. The principle of pacing and leading also applies. If possible, work in your client's own vernacular and don't impose yours on them. It just gets in the way of success.

This means that we must master communication. In other words, to work in our client's own language patterns. Also, to be a credible person when relating to people of different persuasions, class, status and so on.

My wife tells me that the "beauty of me" is that I'm what she calls "intelligent scum" ... I believe this is a term of endearment! What she says is this:

> *"You have three degrees and are at home talking with Professors, Scientists, Politicians, Media people and so on. But you have never lost your working-class accent and earthiness. As a musician, you have also been used to speaking plainly with people in pubs. People don't always get it, but you really are able to reach across a broad church of people."*

This chapter provides an introduction to some of the language structures that can help you get further with your subjects. Remember that language is only 7% of the whole communication message when working face to face. Sure, getting the words right matters but it is not the whole package.

Specifically Vague

NLP talks of two language models. The **Meta Model** and the **Milton Model**:

Meta language patterns are highly specific. Whereas the **Milton** model, named after Milton H. Erickson, is the kind of vague language used by hypnotists, therapists, gaslighters and some Brexit politicians. We can use the meta model to identify and correct deletions, distortions and generalisations through language challenges. It is useful in conducting Brexorcisms being mindful of John Heron's style model. It is also useful for dealing with what are called "gaslighting" incidents where people make statements that are untrue for the purposes of getting others to question their own sanity. Here are some of the main "violations" of clear language patterns with some typical statements that leave voters use in conversations and some meta model challenges of the statements:

Deletions

1. Unspecified Nouns

Conversations with Brexit voters are littered with unspecified nouns. Here are some of the more familiar ones in *italics* with some starting points for responses:

"Get over it."

"What specifically do I need to get over?"

"Out means Out. Can't you get that through your head."

"Which things must I get through my head?"

2. Unspecified Verbs

"Remainers upset me."

"How exactly are you making them upset you?"

"Stop trying to undermine democracy."

"How specifically am I undermining democracy?"

Dealing with Deletion

"Cheese and onion crisps will still be available after No Deal Brexit"

Boris Johnson

On occasion, Brexorcisms are confounded by missing chunks of information. This is what NLP specialists call "deletion". Boris did not tell an untruth in the above example, yet he failed to talk about medicines and the 80% of foodstuffs that we import on a daily basis.

It is entirely possible that cheese and onion crisps are not essential to life ...

This kind of gaslighting only makes it harder for people to find the truth in our politics. The intention is to get people to rise quickly to anger or fight, attack. This is then used to discredit any valid point they may make.

3. Nominalisations

Nominalisations convert a verb to make it a noun. They are often accompanied by the words must, mustn't, have to, should, shouldn't, ought to, can, can't, could, couldn't, would, wouldn't:

"Women have no understanding of politics."

"All women? What don't they understand?"

"We want it all. I want Brex .. it now."

"What Brexity thing do you want?"

"I need sovereignty."

"How do you want to be sovereign?"

"You shouldn't wear the EU flag on your blazer."

"According to whom?"

4. Unspecified Referential Index

A phrase which deletes the person(s) doing the action or which uses a general subject, for example immigrants, Jews, men.

"Eastern Europeans are lazy."

"Which ones? How are they lazy? How do you know?"

"People don't like you going on about Brexit."

"Which people?"

"Muslims stop us having Christmas. I've seen the Muslims, the Bulgarians, they're everywhere."

A word on breathing

Getting our language right is one thing. Developing the other 93% of the dance of persuasive communications right is quite another. A pure focus on the words is rather like a musician just focusing on the sheet music, rather than the performance and the audience ...

Pauses can be very effective in improving your subject's listening. I have even walked away from subjects that don't take turns ...

7% language
38% voice tone
55% body language

Don't forget to breathe when communicating. It also makes a statement ...

Match your subject's body language to improve their attention. Mismatch when you wish to disagree without having to disagree ...

"How do Muslims stop you having Christmas? Where are they? How many Bulgarians are Muslims?"

5. Simple Deletions

"Britain has had problems for a long time, so Brexit is the answer."

"What problems? The answer to what?"

"Brexit is better."

"Better? Than what?"

6. Comparative Deletions

"Britain can be great again."

"Great in what way?"

"We can grow our own vegetables."

"Which vegetables grow in Britain?"

Distortions

7. Complex Equivalence

An attribution of a cause to something that may have no correlation:

"My local chip shop is doing fine. So, Brexit will be OK."

"How is your local chip shop an index of the state of UK industry and macroeconomics?"

"I hate people coming over here and taking our jobs and they're not even working."

"How are they taking our jobs if they don't work?"

"My dad fought in the war, so Brexit would be OK."

Reframing distorted views

The meaning of any communication depends on the "frame" in which we perceive it. Reframing is the process of changing the frame in which a person perceives issues in order to change the meaning. Reframing is a key component of many jokes, fairy tales and Brexit delusions. It is particularly of value when working with limiting beliefs of leave voters, where their frame of reference is limited by perspective, time or just plain wrong.

Vote Leave cleverly reframed the idea of recklessness to ideas about being bold. Whereas David Cameron could only manage to say "I don't believe we are quitters." In NLP terms he was indicating that Remainers were cowards.

Reframes can be simple, trivial or complex and deep.

"The EU are bullying us."

"They must be very concerned about how we are self-harming the country."

"Remainers are killing Britain."

"They must be very organised and intelligent to be able to do such a thing. What do they know?"

Let's talk about BREX .. it

"How is Brexit anything like a war?"

"Brexit will fix the NHS."

"How are Brexit and the NHS related?"

"Brexit means that Britain will improve dramatically."

"In what respects specifically?"

8. Lost Performative

In this conversational conundrum, a value judgment is made without knowing who or what is making the judgement:

"I cannot read graphs and data about Brexit"

"According to whom?"

"A 2nd referendum is anti-democratic."

"Says who?"

"Brexit is good."

"Brexit. What is it good for?"

9. Mind Reading

Claiming to know another's thoughts or feelings without specifying the how you came to that knowledge:

"You are trying to make me look stupid."

"How do you know what I'm trying to do?"

"You know how I feel about Brexit."

"I did not realise you read my mind. Can you explain how you do that?"

Dealing with Brexit Shape Shifters

Ever had this kind of conversation with a Brexiteer?

"Let's talk about your job as a stock controller. You said Brexit was ruining it. I'd love to know the specifics"

"That's one thing, but my boss makes my life hell."

"OK, so let's discuss the boss. Is he European?"

"I don't care about him. He's from Basildon anyway. I can't get an appointment at the hospital due to immigration."

What is stopping you getting an appointment at the hospital?"

"My boss. He says I'm not ill. I just hate this job."

"So, let's focus on the job. You said Brexit was ruining it."

"I'd rather be a bus driver." ….

There is a balance to be struck between letting your subject unload on you for the purposes of venting and just an unfocussed discussion that achieves little. The Meta Model provides you with a wide range of tools for flexibility. However, sometimes you just need to come back to the point:

"You said you wanted to talk about how the EU is ruining your job. Tell me more."

"Let's stick to this subject until we are done."

"Brexit ruins your job. How?"

10. Cause – Effect

In this language game, a direct cause and effect are inferred from disparate items.

"Look what you made me do."

"How exactly did I make you do that?"

"If it weren't for the Remainers, Brexit would be alright now."

"What have the activities of Remainers got to do with the success of Brexit?"

11. Presuppositions

The NLP equivalent of assumptions. It is generally held that assumptions make an ASS out of U and ME (see what I did there?).

"Anti-Brexit protestors cause wars."

"How do peaceful protests cause wars?"

"Women manipulate men to give into Remaining."

"Are all women manipulative? No man ever is?"

Generalisations

12. Universal Quantifiers

These are generalisations without a reference point. Frequently such statements include all, every, none, never etc.

"Theresa May's a Remainer all the time."

"So, Theresa May never argues for Brexit?"

Dealing with Generalisations

We generalise all the time. Life would be too difficult to endure without using some generalisations to get through every day. Some generalisations are safe and without consequence, for example the generalisation that all cities are busy helps us plan extra time to cross Central London. Just occasionally we are wrong about how busy London will be, but this usually comes without serious consequence.

Our earlier example of the Irish immigrant who told my wife that our local Council was to house **ALL** the London Borough refugees is a good example of a generalisation. It may in part be true, but he had quickly moved from a specific to a general. Generalisations litter the Brexit voter's landscape:

"Everyone in the town wants Brexit."

"Everyone?"

"Brexit was the will of the people."

"Which people? What is Brexit?"

Let's talk about BREX .. it

"No one wants to alter the course of fate."

"No-One? What is fate?"

13. Modal Operators of Necessity

Words that require actions e.g. should, shouldn't, must, mustn't, have to, need to etc.

"We must carry on with Brexit."

"Must we? Who said we must? What would happen if we didn't?"

"We must not interfere with democracy."

"How are we interfering with democracy? What is democracy?"

14. Modal Operators of Possibility

Words that imply no choice e.g. can't, haven't, won't etc.

"I can't tell you the truth about immigration."

"What would happen if you did?"

"I won't change my mind on Brexit."

"What prevents you from changing your mind in the light of new knowledge?

Thinking about Brexorcism

Reflect on the Meta Model language patterns using this stream of consciousness from a leave voter below.

- Identify the various language patterns inherent in the conversation.

- Where are the opportunities for intervention?

- Where would you begin?

We are an island, tunnel or no tunnel, and if it comes to war, the tunnel will go. If the EU and Paris play sufficiently silly buggers, to the point it becomes militarily necessary, we can always pull the plug on the tunnel and flood it. In a war scenario, I don't think we'd be too bothered about compensating Paris or shareholders. The Armed Forces are largely pro-Brexit, even in Scotland. England and Wales are not in doubt. All the army people would love to get involved in a war with France, Germany and the other EU nations.

And we could take back control of our railways. The East Coast Main Line worked well under the real LNER (1923-47), complete with the setting of a speed record in 1938 which stands to this day. Go back to the Big Four or pre-grouping model, where TOCs owned their railways. It worked very well. Southern Railway coaches were a lovely shade of green and carriages were made of wood. German railways survive only on subsidy from Britain. SNCF is bankrupt.

Let's talk about BREX .. it

Old Age Brexiteers speak out ...

Some people are a mixed bag of tricks. They don't fit into just one of our meta model categories. Here is a particularly difficult example with what I call OABs (Old Age Brexiteers). How would you tackle the person involved:

A female friend of mine posted this on social media:

"I've just realised that my pension will be worthless after Brexit."

It is possible that she voted to leave and has just realised that it will affect her badly.

A mutual acquaintance posted this reply (grammar and spelling left as posted):

"Your pension will be worth it worth ... Having worked in the major banking sector ... in black Wednesday ...I do not understand your worries . Yes, this a weather report but we the brittish people will win so tell your MP.s that unless they stand with us"

I am quite sure that this person has never worked in any significant position in a bank if that provides some reassurance by the way. There is a deletion in here "will be worth it worth", plus a host of other meta model violations. Any possible resolution is made much worse. as the post is on social media. Therefore, it cannot be guaranteed that a communications channel actually exists, that the person will listen to any answers and so on ...

Your reflections:

The **Meta Model** has been extended by the originators Bandler and Grinder. However, I feel this is quite enough for an introduction to the topic. I will leave discussions on the illusion of choice, delusional thinking, pseudo words and so on to the politicians and perhaps an update of this first book on the topic of Brexorcism subject to feedback on the usefulness of this guide.

In contrast, the **Milton Model** derives from Milton H. Erickson, a therapist who used hypnotic language patterns and looser language postulates to help his subjects make dramatic changes. Milton language patterns are very vague. Politicians and some rock stars like ambiguity for different reasons:

Take Back Control

Simply the best

Breaking point

Whole lotta love

Brexit Means Brexit

The winner takes it all

In our Abba example, who is the winner? What is being taken? Is all everything? What is all? Is it all the sausages, the seats on the train, the Brexit benefits or what? Who lost as a result of them winning, and so on …

In the case of the Dominic Cummings "Take Back Control" catchphrase, I've had many a conversation where it becomes embarrassingly apparent that people have no idea as to what is being taken back. They don't actually know what control has been lost, when, who caused it and so on. However, the fact that people repeat the phrase in the same way as they might sing a chant at a football match is testament to the hypnotic power of these gaslighting phrases.

Some hypnotic Milton language patterns are shown below, so that you may spot them and neutralise them when appropriate as part of your "Defence Against the Dark Brexit Arts" strategy.

Let's talk about BREX .. it

Hypnotic language patterns

"Brexit will create new understandings."

"David Cameron made me to vote for Brexit."

"People can change their minds on Brexit."

"No deal is better."

"Your perception of Brexit is changing, isn't it."

"Do you want to have Brexit now or later?"

"Would you rather have Brexit or shall I torch you with a hot flame?"

"It's my deal or no deal."

"It's now or never."

"I will not suggest to you that Brexit is easy."

"It's important we get on with Brexit before time runs out like sand."

"It's essential to save Britain from immigrants."

"You are feeling sleepy as you listen to me talking about Brexit."

I'm not sure which eyelid will close first as you hear me reading Article 50."

"Others cannot say whether Brexit will happen now or later."

"Enough is enough."

"Brexit means Brexit"

Let's talk about BREX .. it

It is an interesting reflection to note that the vast majority of the leave campaign slogans were essentially hypnotic language patterns. They were completely consonant to the voters, playing to things they already thought or had heard and building upon these illusions. For example:

For people who did not like immigration and immigrants, the idea that the entire population of Turkey would invade the UK was a powerful anchor.

For those who felt that the country had lost its way, the idea of taking back control was extremely powerful.

For those who felt that the NHS had been brought to the point of destruction, the idea of giving large sums of money back to the NHS from the EU was another supremely powerful idea. This is part of what is known as "gaslighting", using things that are near and dear to people's hearts to persuade them. Theresa May recently promised £20.4 billion for the NHS over 5 years. When you compare the numbers, it is clear that the promise was a lie although this announcement has been spun as one of honouring the referendum promise.

Promise: £350 million per week

Reality: £20.4 bn over 5 years is £78 million per week. About 1/5 of the promise

In contrast, much of the Remain campaign was spent on specifics and "project fear". These messages were quite dissonant to people that already believed the Vote Leave generalisations and who did not like what they saw as negative messaging.

Like it or loathe it, voters preferred messages that appeared to be consonant with their own beliefs. They also preferred positive hallucinations of the benefits of leaving the EU and gross exaggerations of the perceived problems of staying in the EU.

Much of the persuasive strategies of the Vote Leave campaign can be explained using the Milton Model and the ideas of Deletion, Distortion and Generalisation.

A word on integrity

Tools and techniques will take you so far in the dance of influence and persuasion. Without heart and soul, you ain't got nothin' …

Donald Trump, Nigel Farage and Boris Johnson have great technique as orators, but seemingly no moral compass to temper their words. Thus, their strategies are ultimately morally and practically bankrupt …

In the words of Annie Lennox:

**ptcounty*Be yourself tonight.*

And Lou Reed:

I do me better than anyone else.

I use NLP language skills on a regular basis in my pub and café Brexit conversations. Usually people come to me to talk, triggered by my selection of provocative anti-Brexit T-Shirts. Getting people to want to talk to you rather than the other way round is by far the best way to engage them. Here's a shortened story of one successful interaction with a hardened Brexit voter in "Brexit Central" aka North Kent that illustrates some of these principles in action:

We're goin' down the pub

Oh my ... one-hour Brexit conversation in a pub in Gillingham started by my T-shirt ... 66-year OAB (Old Age Brexiteer) ex BBC radio engineer, two kids, one in Parkhurst the other on the dole ... key points:

"I love your T-shirt, it's very clear, FU ... K BREXIT."

I explain (at great length and very slowly) "yes, FU ... K BREXIT, says it straight, unlike our lying politicians on all sides" yada yada. He nods in agreement ... (pacing).

5 minutes later I have to tell him that we are on different sides as he has not worked it out ... but he agrees and we continue ... (leading).

We covered all kinds of things ... being invaded by the infidel ... the need to get our country back ... the future of life with Trump ... the fact that Vietnam is not in Europe (he did not know and I made the mistake of saying that not many people in the high street would know that ... he then admitted that he did not actually know where Vietnam was).

Eventually after he had "unloaded" on me, I said that it seemed that he really regretted the decline of British industry, he wanted his son to come out of prison and we needed to get back being an island (he had never travelled). I went on to agree with his sense of disappointment and then asked what part of his sense of alienation was due to the EU. The subject changed. After a while he started to talk about his grandchildren. I asked him what he thought we would get from leaving the EU and when. He really did not know.

Let's talk about BREX .. it

Talked about his kids and grandchildren. His daughter is 33, has never worked. His son is older, in Parkhust High Security prison (I do not ask him why his son is there). He does not like his son in Parkhurst because "It's full of blacks", although he is quick to point out that he is not a racist.

He moved away from London because of the blacks 19 years ago and now finds them invading his town. This is the fault of the EU. I point out that immigration is under our own government's control … he agrees … I spend some time trotting out the story of my sister and the two million rapists coming from Berlin. I ask him why rapists from Berlin are "worse" than "great British rapists" … he does not know …

We carry on with kids. I tell him that my son will be 75 by the time we've paid for Brexit.

He nods … there was a lot of nodding … (leading).

Subject changed towards food for some reason … he told me how much he hated all the food in the high street because it had garlic in it. He did not like garlic. I pointed out that it grows here and summed up the lengthy conversation by saying:

"So, if you were to explain to your grandchildren that we were leaving the EU because you don't like garlic and that they would be paying for this for the rest of their lives, would that be enough for them to agree with you?"

His reply "Not really – I'd need another dozen reasons …"

I asked "and what are those?" He did not know …

I considered I had done enough to move him at this point. We changed to talk about music and beer …

Let's talk about BREX .. it

Gaslighting unplugged

Gaslighting is a form of manipulation whose purpose is to cause the victim to doubt their own perception, memory and sanity; to destabilise.

In November 2018 Theresa May said that her Brexit deal was in the national interest six times and that her deal delivers on everything she promised seven times.

"If a little bit of Guinness is smuggled over the border, I don't mind."

Jacob Rees-Mogg on the Irish border.

"Lock her up."

Donald Trump on Hilary Clinton.

Final remarks

I could go on at length about the question of style and whether you should use more directive or non-directive approaches, the gentle art and discipline of storytelling, body language, challenging viewpoints without tears and so on. We have already discussed some of these issues and getting the language right is but part of any successful Brexorcism. Authenticity wins ultimately in the game of influence and persuasion, but people are sometimes taken in by some snappy lines. In the words of Nick Clegg:

"If it sounds too good to be true, it probably is."

Summary

- The Meta and Milton Models can help you spot the language patterns in conversations you have with potential Brexorcism candidates. Having spotted the language patterns that others use, you can then intervene skilfully. They also help you understand your own values, beliefs and behaviours.
- People do not operate in one mode at any one time. The models help you to adapt your own behaviour in a given interaction. Flexibility is key to success.
- Begin by identifying your own language patterns as a start. By improving your own awareness, you will equip yourself to help others challenge their own habits and thinking traps.
- Remember that, whilst getting your language right, our body language and voice tone also make up the communication message. Learn to use these well.
- Act with integrity if you want to be influential.

What should the Remain Campaign do with NLP in a People's Vote or General Election?

Quite a lot. Remain lost the referendum due to a brilliant campaign by Vote Leave and a lacklustre strategy by the Remain side. There is plenty to learn, but here is a taste of what must be done should the need arise:

Find better mantras: Remain is a weak concept and sounded dull to leavers. Our suggestion of "Better Britain, Better Europe, Better World" is positive but perhaps long. It can however be reduced to Better Britain. "Remain and Reform" is also a more useful catchphrase than "Remain", as the reform element respects the concerns of leave voters from 2016.

Kick ass: Lacklustre and long messages do not reach busy people or ones with lower general intelligence. The Remain campaign's wishes to be in the quality newspapers ignores the fact that leave voters tend not to read them. Love it or loathe it, the phrase "Take Back Control" captured the zeitgeist of those who felt left behind.

KISS: Keep it simple stupid. To reach some demographics Remain needs much simpler and more hard-hitting messaging. Remain may loathe Nigel Farage but we need to learn from him. Our language and messages must reach Sun readers, like it or not.

Facts or Fantasies: Facts were considered project fear last time. Now that we have experience, we can point to facts about what Brexit will look like. We should challenge Brexit fantasies with facts whilst dealing with the question of why Remain and Reform gives us better futures.

Emotions win: Remain's campaign was unemotional last time. We need to get personal this time.

PART II

Skills and Stories

Chapter I

Dance, Music, Sex, Romance ... and Brexit

This chapter has an inaccurate title. There is no discussion of dance as a medium of Defence Against the Dark Brexit Arts here. But, just like Brexit, I'm not concerned about letting the truth get in the way of a good title and story ...

However, whilst we are on the subject of sex, in July 2016 I made the slightly tongue in cheek suggestion that Remain voting women should deny their Brexit husbands certain ... er ... sensual benefits ... This was not an idle suggestion. We know that the Brexit vote was a triumph of the visceral senses over logic. In this same vein, the supply (or denial) of other "basic instincts" may well have been more effective than asking partners to read articles or graphs in the intelligent press. As a male in a politically correct age, I cannot possibly go further in offering practical advice on this subject, so I must leave it to your imagination ...

But since we are on this subject, the conversation must surely turn eventually from sex to love and affection. Whilst we have focused on the importance of language and techniques to turn minds, we must not ignore what Kate Bush would call "The Sensual Brexit World", as this story from a female friend illustrates:

Sexual Brexit Healing

A very good friend of mine voted to leave. I had been going on about how thick people must have been to vote in that way and he admitted that he had. When challenged, he said "because I'm a patriot and I love my country". Around this time, he was single but meeting various ladies online, mostly in Scandinavia. We asked him how that would work out if there were no planes after Brexit, he looked shocked. Since then, he has met a lovely German lady who lives in Bavaria. They got married this weekend in Denmark! He has completely changed his mind. He has promised me that he will return to vote remain if there is a second referendum.

Love changes everything ...

Let's talk about BREX .. it

Turning away from sex, and sidestepping romance, our next logical step is music, by the process of elimination, or just random selection! The philosopher Emmanuel Kant (and Madonna) pointed out that music is the language of the emotions. As such, music has the potential to reach the minds of Brexit voters via their hearts. It is also an artform that is particularly relevant towards mass communication, reaching people in groups. Many remain campaigners have tried to reach more than one person at a time, via public speaking, poetry, performance art and music. I'd like to take some time here to expound the benefits and limitations of these artforms.

Music has huge advantage compared with other media, as it has rhythm, rhyme and the potential to reach people's emotional core. In my professional life I can attest to this when I travel round the world speaking. I speak with business audiences and sometimes find it hard to get them to recall what their business idols have said about critical business issues. However, wherever I am in the world, I find it easy to get business people to recite the words to Bohemian Rhapsody, even though the song is over 40 years old. They should really know more of Freddie Herzberg's lyrics than Freddie Mercury! Our Bohemian Rhapsody story is, of course, is only one example, but it seems that music reaches us in ways that beats many other things. This explains the power of music to change minds. Music has been used in all kinds of contexts, from trivia such as "boy meets girl" pop songs, as a call to action for protest, to inspire people to work harder and in major global social campaigns such as in Live Aid and so on.

Set against that, much music is in the eye of the beholder. Put simply, what I like in music is down to my own taste. If you don't like it, you are at liberty to have that view. When we tried to music as a mass communication device to protest about Brexit, we found that people felt that they had to like a song in order to get behind a particular cause. So, if we produced a pop song, some would like it and others would consider it lightweight and ask for rock or rap. If we then made a rock song, we'd get the opposite series of complaints. It was difficult to separate the project (stopping Brexit) from the process (musical preferences and in some cases musical snobbery). I note with some dispassion that people don't apply the same levels of scrutiny to an anti-Brexit Facebook meme, a sticker, T-shirt etc. This both illustrates the power of music and its limitations as an artform. It probably accounts for the reason why Bob Geldof said "just buy the fu..king song" when he organised Live Aid. We will illustrate some of the successes and failures of the more exotic approaches to Brexit activism in coming chapters.

The love I lost

In October 2015, I started doing some occasional freelance work in the civil service as an internal communications filmmaker. They liked what I did and asked me back to undertake many other shoots. The following March, one department decided they wanted a full-time position with me in mind. A position went up on the Civil Service Jobs website and I was one of more than 230 who applied. I was told in the week running up to the referendum that I was on a shortlist of 10, but that was a formality as they preferred me out of the others. Basically, the job was as good as mine and the official interview (to be confirmed after the referendum result) was an open door.

But this assumed that the Remain side would win, and no changes had to be made inside. I'm obliged not to say what those changes were. But any interview was put on hold, leaving me in limbo. Barely weeks later, the job listing had been taken off the website, leading me to assume the position had been taken. But my colleagues later confirmed that the position was one of 60 jobs which had been cancelled due to Brexit.

When people tell you that Brexit won't affect people, there are thousands of small examples like this. Uncertainty produces stasis and risk averse decisions.

Let's talk about BREX .. it

Chapter II
Brexit Oddity

"Ground control to Theresa May
Take your HRT and put your heels away"

At the outset of my Brexit resistance I worked with the No 10 Vigil who faithfully stood outside No 10 Downing Street three nights every week, delivering performance art, traditional protest and talking to passers-by about Brexit. All of us were quite inexperienced at street protest. In my case, I had never done such a thing in my life. It was a great privilege to help start the resistance movement and I met some great people at the Vigil, pioneered and led by Diane Datson. These include various partners in crime: Jane Berry, William Harrison, Susanna Leissle, Charlie Grosvenor, Drew Galdron, Amanda Radford, Judith Spencer, Richard Smith, Paolo Arrigo, Bruce Tanner, Michela Bertaglia, Jenna Efkay, The SNP, Wendy Nowak, An Vrancken, Emmy Van Deurzen, Katy Treverton, Jon Danzig, Richard Steeden, Erwin Schaefer, Martin Housden, Gareth Steel, Peter Jordan, Mike Galsworthy, Heather Styles, Sam Powell, Steve Bray and many more.

It quickly became obvious that we needed to use the diverse talents to best effect in order to project our "Voices for Europe". In my case, I have a skill at twisting traditional songs and turning them into Brexit satire. One such example is that of David Bowie's "Space Oddity", which we turned into a tale of Brexit and space discovery. I mused upon the fact that Brexit is rather like going into space, but without all the usual risk management devices, oxygen, food, fuel, medicines and so on. I've reproduced Bowie's warped words over the page. I also know that David Bowie had a terrific sense of ironic humour and drama. I hope in some small way that he might have enjoyed this deeply satirical rewrite of his classic.

To perform satire on a busy street is quite hard. One is competing with London street noise, sirens, heckling, short attention spans, occasional polite visits by the Metropolitan Police and so on. So, it is really important to gain rapport with your audience and explain what you are about to do, especially since Bowie was only recently dead when we started doing these performances. In such circumstances, satire can quickly turn to offence for your audience. Having worked with a few rock stars, I know too well about fragile egos and why they often avoid contact with their fans.

Let's talk about BREX .. it

Preparation is vital to get your message across in such circumstances. Therefore, I often set this piece up via a dialogue with the audience using the following general approach:

- I begin by pointing out in a deeply ironic way that Bowie was a visionary, starting from humble beginnings in Bromley (the big question really was whether Bromley South or Bromley North had the best train service). After spending several years in a monastery (necessary after writing "The Laughing Gnome"), Bowie turned to space travel for inspiration.

- I then suggest (tongue in cheek) that Bowie's lyric to Space Oddity foreshadowed Brexit by some 45 years. Or perhaps he was just mindless on drugs and the lyrics just fell that way due to Bowie's use of the "cut-up" approach derived from the Beat Movement ...

- I sometimes qualify all the above by publicly stating my love for Bowie's music, having been asked to speak about his life on CNN on the sad day of his untimely death. This helps deal with some of the assumptions that people may hold about a satirical performance of a classic.

I consider taking the lyrics of a recently deceased pop icon in vain to be a high-risk strategy. The fact that we have never had people complaining but more often had people singing along to the song is testimony to the Bananrama quote "It ain't what you do, it's the way that you do it." It really all depends on the preparation. I always take a little time to speak with the audience beforehand to bring them into the piece. This included a performance at Bowie's memorial in Brixton, almost a sacred shrine. This strategy has always worked well, much to many people's surprise.

When we've done the song in pubs, the most important aspect of the performance are the conversations that take place after this cathartic release of energy. These range from "great song" and other unimportant stuff, through to "what do you think about Brexit?" Once that question has been asked, you know that people are ready to receive in terms of our model of communications. Music and other strategies can be effective icebreakers to what has almost become an undiscussable item in polite English conversation.

Let's talk about BREX .. it

Check the versions of the song out at The Bank of England, 10 Downing Street and other places at our YouTube channel. Also, via Norwegian TV via www.tv2no/a/10274532

Brexit Oddity …

Let's talk about BREX .. it

Brexit Oddity

Ground Control to Theresa May x 2
Take your HRT and put your heels away

Ground Control to Theresa May
Something else that rhymes with Theresa May (hay – invite audience participation)
Check ignition and may Brexit be with you

This is Ground Control to Theresa May
You've really made the grade
And the papers want to know whose pants you wear (the leather ones)
Now it's time to leave the EU if you dare

This is Theresa May to Ground Control
I'm stepping through the door at Dover (it takes seven hours after Brexit)
And I'm floating in a strong and stable way
And the stars look very different today

For here am I sitting in my white van (usually a white van passes)
Far above the EU
The Planet Earth is blue and there's nothing I can do

Though I'm past one hundred thousand miles I'm feeling very still
And I think my Brexit spaceship knows which way to go (I asked David Davis, although he's a bit of a tw..t)
Tell Jeremy Corbyn "I love him very much, he knows"

Ground Control to Theresa May Your circuit's dead, there's something wrong
Can you hear me, Theresa May? x 3 (shouts at microphone "You're not listening love")
Can you...

Here am I sitting in my white van
Far above the EU
The Planet Earth is blue and there's nothing I can do

Thinking about Brexorcism

Reflect on the Space Oddity story for your own campaigning.

What could you do in your area that engages people better?

The Brexitometers are a great tool of engagement for three reasons:

- They offer people meaningful participation in issues that affect their lives. The act of voting on the street is a rehearsal for a better form of democracy.

- They offer opportunities for 1:1 conversations, as per our stories in this book.

- They demonstrate trust in politics which is sadly lacking. If someone wants to vote on the leave side, we encourage them to do so.

How can you bring more people to street stalls via art, music and so on?

Could you arrange "Question Time" events in your area?

How about concerts and social events? Especially ones that reach demographics that Remain campaigners do not reach? Non-Voters, Leavers in regret, Soft Leavers, Remainers in remission etc.

Can you arrange newsworthy events in your area with quality journalism attached to the event?

Chapter III
Isas, Isis and Brexit

I spend a lot of time talking to Brexit supporters in pubs. Why? Because the environment allows for a non-confrontational atmosphere in which to have what are often "difficult conversations". The conversations have only become potentially aggressive a couple of times out of many attempts, so they are generally low risk. However, one must keep one's temper, sometimes against the odds of some breath-taking revelations. One such revelation came from a pub landlord who told me he wanted to get rid of all the ISAs. In case you are confused.com, an ISA is an Individual Savings Product. Of course, what he meant was ISIS. In other words that all Moslems in the UK were members of terrorist cells. An important difference from savings products!

Here are some snippets from a recording I made of the Brexit Pub Landlord. You can find the "Brexit Monologue" interviews on YouTube in their entirety. Go to youtube.com/academyofrock and then look for the "Politics and Business" playlist.

On laws, hoovers and saving the planet

"I tell you what … You can't have a hoover over a thousand Watts …"

"Isn't that a good law, to stop us killing the planet?"

"I don't care about the planet. I just wanna have a powerful hoover."

On human rights and game boys

"I tell you what … What about the human rights law?"

"Yes, it's a good thing?"

"It ain't. Bloody prisoners, done rape and all that. They give 'em game boys. We should bring back hanging."

Chapter IV
Suffer Little Children

I attended Parliament Square on the day of Theresa May's "meaningful vote". For some two and a half years we had hardly seen a Vote Leave activist on the street, but recent events had caused a few of them to turn up. It transpired that a few of them were "paid hands' to boost numbers, but however ...

The typical tactic of the "Yellow Vests" in UK is to walk through the Remain protest to incite trouble. The standard response is no response, so that we keep good relations with the Metropolitan Police who look after us at such events.

A gathering of Vote Leave people had formed inside our protest and Police were surrounding them ... Yellow Vests on Yellow Vests! I was on the outside of the circle, standing next to a woman who had been marching with a young child, perhaps eight years old, both in Yellow Vests, shouting and swearing. I decided to set aside my personal views about the wisdom of teaching her eight-year-old daughter to F and C at her fellow citizens and wonder why she was not at school.

After a while I said to her casually: "I wish I had 1:1 bodyguards like you lot do. It's great!"

She looked surprised: "They are not bodyguards! Why would you want them with you?"

I opened my phone and pulled up The Daily Mirror article. I showed her and her daughter the picture, saying: "Well, this is what people like this do to me."

I paused whilst they looked in horror and worked out what might have happened ...

There was visible shock. The daughter did not realise the picture was me. Eventually she said: "Is that you?" I nodded. Her mum said: "We don't do that to people."

I said: "I know you don't, but that's what your people have invited in through the side door ..." I was mindful of the fact that a minor was with us, so I kept my contributions brief and reasonably light, but firm. After all, the mother had taken her daughter out of school to an "adult event" but I considered it unhelpful to force my points home.

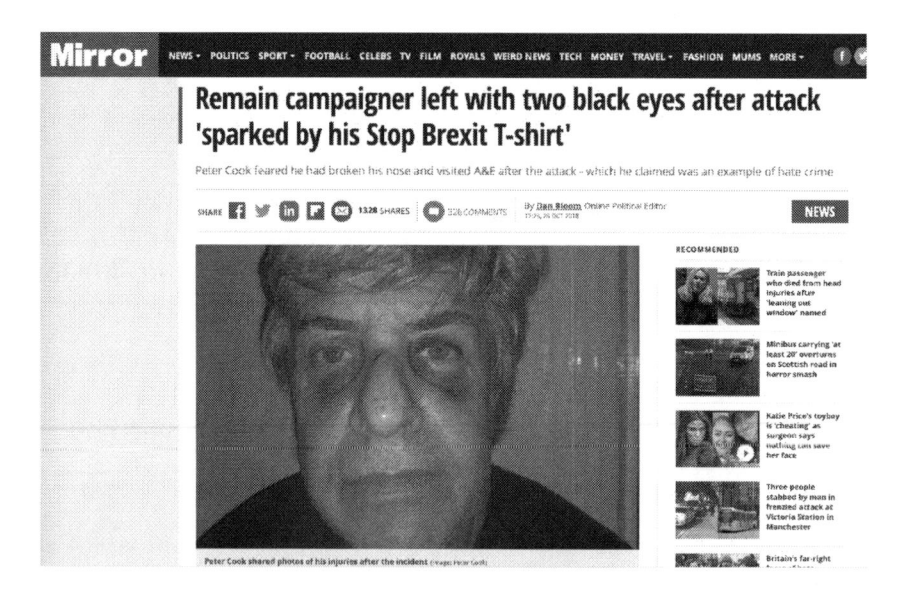

Mirror — Remain campaigner left with two black eyes after attack 'sparked by his Stop Brexit T-shirt'

Peter Cook feared he had broken his nose and visited A&E after the attack – which he claimed was an example of hate crime

Her husband noticed me and walked over. The daughter related the story to him (much better than me repeating it). Once he heard the story he pronounced: "Ah, this will be George Soros behind this. He pays people to do this to people like you."

I looked puzzled and said: "So, you were there then? You seem to know more about it than I do?" Silence …

After some small talk we all shook hands. I'm left wondering what questions the daughter will have had around the dinner table that evening and at school …

Reflections on my strategy

- This was a good example of mostly non-directive interventions using "co-operative" and "autonomous" modes mostly in John Heron terms.

- Silence was a key component of the strategy.

- The exception was a confrontation strategy when I challenged the husband's attempt at mind reading with his George Soros remark.

Chapter V
No wonder you're fed up

Awkward reflection ...

I've been thinking about the complaints of Brexiteers who feel left behind and who have a sense of entitlement about our place in the world and their right to a comfortable life in a global world ... Brexit has called into question so many fundamental issues and made me think about the meaning of life and so on. In this "awkward personal reflection", I muse upon life's contradictions and complexities. I ask you to do the same ...

I am first a business person who believes that life is what you make it. I am equally first someone who believes that capitalism has gone too far when a few people live in gated communities and public servants have to go to food banks in order to live. I don't therefore fit into trivial bipolar notions of left or right and there is a bit of every political party running through my veins ... In short, I am an adventure capitalist with heart and a belief that we don't solve world problems through short-termism and unsustainable practices. The Conservative party in its current form have no answers to the malaises of the 4th industrial age. In extremis, the wickedness of the hard right of the Tory party leads us to a socially and morally bankrupt world. On the other hand, Labour's romanticism of a return to a fantasy land where every village has a Spinning Jenny, a blacksmith, tailor, butcher, baker etc. and the workhouse are equally at odds with my values of self-determination ...

But, surprisingly, even I have the same human faults designed into me as everyone else! I was thinking about the plight of those who voted for Brexit because they were angry or felt left behind after extensive pub / café conversations and I'm ashamed to say that I had the underlying thought that they kind of deserve Brexit. They will get more exploitation, more minimum wage gigs, less worker's rights and so on in a deregulated Britain - out of the Brexit frying pan into Trump's fire, so to speak. All whilst the disaster capitalists get richer and the gap between rich and poor widens. Importantly, if Brexit happens, those migrants that we have exploited on farms, in service industries and on arse wiping duties in care homes will have gone home, leaving those jobs for the unwilling and lazy Brits. At the same time, those people working in knowledge-based industries are always going to be the most mobile in the 4th industrial age. Our doctors, computing experts, engineers, scientists, vets etc. will find more productive arenas to flex their collective synapses and so on ...

As a knowledge worker myself, I have always worked internationally and even at my advanced age I feel able to ride the waves of Brexit by redirecting myself more towards international markets, leaving Brexit Britain to become a land of low skill, low wage, high exploitation jobs for a passive workforce that wanted their country back and a 50p pound ...

They are welcome to it ... today I just begun explorations about seeking a mortgage to give my children some foundations whilst giving considerations towards securing Irish citizenship as a strategy to mitigate against the self-harming behaviour of 27% of the "Great British people."

Big Questions for Little England

- Am I wrong to feel a sense of outrage with my fellow citizens, including one or two family members?

- Does capitalism need fundamental reform for the 4th industrial age?

- Do we now have the means to introduce greater citizen democracy? Could we foresee an age when we have red button democracy via our televisions or smartphones? Just because we can, should we do this?

- Is the answer to wealth to pull everyone down to be poor?

- Is the answer to poverty to give everyone the means to be rich?

- What are your questions?

Brexit Reflections

Chapter VI
The Brexit punch bowl

I was unfortunate in so far that I got punched by seven angry Brexiteers shortly after the October 2018 People's March. The story was reported as widely as Norwegian TV alongside The Sun, Mail, BBC Radio and TV. It turns out that tensions were heightened in the days following that march and quite a few people suffered violence at the hands of a few extremists. Check out Norwegian TV at www.tv2no/a/10274532

It would be all too easy to become a victim at this point. I have had so many people either saying that "I deserved it for being a traitor" or presuming that I would stop putting myself at risk. People rightly fear personal attacks. To be honest, it was not the best day of my life! I had previously assumed that people of advanced years were somehow immune to violence from youths in gangs. Clearly not.

But there are several mistakes that must not be made here:

1. To assume that such things are widespread and therefore to stop campaigning to end Brexit populism. My experience was the **exception**, not the norm. I have a bicycle with a large hoarding that says "Break Brexit Before Brexit Breaks Britain" on it and T-Shirts that say the same. My phone has a Boll..cks to Brexit sticker on the back, which is always visible in cafés etc. I do this as I know that these act as incredibly effective icebreakers to restarting the conversation about Brexit with tired Remainers and leavers in regret / denial. I don't wish to agree with the Daily Mail readers that say "I deserve my fate". However, I make myself highly visible and this makes me more of a target than the average person. It **does not mean** that others will suffer the same fate. I live in a Brexity area as well. I also refuse to be silenced by a very small nasty element which has always existed in English society and which has been empowered by our Brexit referendum.

2. To assume that this behaviour will go away if we ignore it. Ignoring bad behaviour is a classic way to extinguish it but the genie is out of the bottle on this and we have a far right which is quietly stoking such behaviour by a few people.

3. To assume that this behaviour will get worse if we withdraw Article 50 and / or stop Brexit. Fear is a powerful motivator, but the statistics don't match people's feelings in this area. Just this weekend, some 100 "Yellow Jackets" demonstrated in London and some other cities, targeting Greggs the bakers for vegan Sausage rolls ... I'm still having trouble understanding the relevance to Brexit but that may just go to show that I'm something of a "pastry elitist". But let's also put the numbers in perspective. 100 protestors and 4 arrests. Compare with some 840 000 people attending The People's March in October 2018 with no trouble and no arrests.

Shortly after my attack I wrote to Gina Miller with my reflections on our new binary choice:

1. CARRY ON with Brexit and normalise misogynism, xenophobia, racism and hate back into Britain as part of the Little England culture.

2. STOP Brexit and possibly have a weekend of riots from a few extremists. We can then begin the journey back to a civil society and a Better Britain in a Better Europe for a Better World. In doing so, we could begin to address the root causes of the referendum result rather than the symptoms.

Yet, some of the feedback from The Daily Mail, The Sun, Mirror and my local newspaper makes for interesting reading. There is no greater fear than fear itself. Do not be seduced into thinking that an end to Brexit will breed a new generation of thugs. We still have the same number of thugs that we always had. Many of them are too busy watching the X-Factor rather than worrying about the BreX-Factor!

Medway Messenger

Angry of Chatham wrote:

Has this guy got a job? (Sounds not as he has not mentioned having to take time off work for his injuries) If not he should lose his benefits as he is not making himself available for work. Sounds like a drain on society. Loser.

Editors' note: There was no mention of any of this. Total fabrication.

Let's talk about BREX .. it

tideyd01 wrote:

Brilliant illustration of what is wrong with Brexit. Who would want to be associated with people who think it's alright to beat someone up for wearing a t-shirt. Compare that with the good nature amongst the 700,000 who marched in London for a second vote. Nasty, snarling hatred is definitely a trait of the right wing as so often demonstrated by the ugly, racist nationalism demonstrated by a lot of contributors to this site. Did you see the pro Brexit supporters deliberately delaying an ambulance with its lights and sirens going on Westminster Bridge did you ? Like to stick up for that would you ?

pip wrote:

We had a vote. Leave won 52 to 48 so that's it. Get over it. If it had been the other way I'm sure it would have been all forgotten by now. You can't have another vote because it will destroy people's faith in democracy. If we have a vote and remain win, will we have the best of 3? It's really getting to much now. Man up and take the result. We may not like it but that's what the majority wanted. Surely we are not that gullible to believe all the scaremongering. When anything goes wrong in future e.g. shares drop,interest rates go up,bad weather , it's will be Brexit's fault. Before Brexit we never had black Monday. We never had big high street shops disappear. We lost our car industry to Europe. Must of been Brexit. Who owns edf Dartford crossing, royal mail the railways? It's definately isn't British. Is that the fault of the leavers vote?

scott wrote:

Simple..Dont wear the shirt! You know what your doing, so how your surprised by repercussions is beyond me...

The Daily Mail

Lone263, Edmon, Canada

The left finally getting theirs!

Editor's note: interesting assumption

nostalgic, Leicestershire, United Kingdom

Don't condone the violence, but people generally do not like other people views bring thrust in their face. If someone went around with JC's mug on their T shirt, I'd want to throw things at it.

Panda2018, Chengdu, China

Not right to be treated like this in a supposedly democratic country, however the hairstyle could be exacerbating the situation.

Let's talk about BREX .. it

Teresa, BRIDGEND

His t shirt doesn't bother me, however, that hair???

Punkawallah, Chandigarh, United Kingdom

He should probably know better at his age?

RobbRaw, Hammersmith London, United Kingdom

Doubt it was just his t shirt that sparked abuse, find some remoaners cannot accept the democratic outcome, and demand a block, or reversal without a debate. That or the mindset, have more referendums until the silly people vote stay.

Bazzy, London, United Kingdom

I fear there will be much more of this violence if the Bexit voters are denied the democracy they were promised in the original vote in June 16.

Alexander, Brackley, United Kingdom

This is wrong poor man ...... However this may happen on a huge scale if the government try to force another referendum the country could end up in anarchy. We must follow the will of the people and democracy

Garry Latjion, London, United Kingdom

not statistically representative enough. Make an experiment in at least 20 towns

billyelton, Peterborough, United Kingdom

So the young don't want Brexit , that shows you how strong the anti EU feeling is right around the country , interfere with it at your peril !

Duckylady, Cambs

Never thought I might fear for my life and that of my children in Britain. We will go to Germany on 27th March to watch Brexit from a safe distance. Remember Yugoslavia 1991. I really hope it doesn't happen here, but not willing to take a chance with my family's lives. Can't deny there is a lot of hate already and many warning signs. Civilisation is but a thin veneer, and torn away all too easily.

Sobieski III, Chester, United Kingdom

Oh dear. Try not to wear that tee shirt next time your out

Let's talk about BREX .. it

Katieconker, Hornchurch, United Kingdom

Despite what we are force fed by the remainers, there's a lot of strong feeling for Brexit out there. Best to keep viewpoints private!

Curtis, London, United Kingdom

Don't ware the silly T shirt then.

MUtowin, Not London, United Kingdom

Things that didn't happen.

Youranidiot1, No mans land, United Kingdom

I highly doubt this happened.

Tim Fixit, Barrybados

Knowing how much the Brexit issue angers people on both sides of the argument the last thing I would do is go around draped in slogans like that for either side. Keep it to yourself man.

TooMuchTyme, Surrey, United Kingdom

There is no justification for violence. However, this man is wearing a t-shirt that supports stripping people of their democratic vote. That is understandably going to irk people.

Ms Wise one, Beaconsfield, United Kingdom

Brexit is the best thing for Britain especially a managed no deal.

BBI3, London, United Kingdom

Its not an anti-brexit t shirt. Its an anti democracy t shirt.

I190, London, United Kingdom

Violence is not acceptable, ever, but I doubt he was innocent his agitation of these situations. He is stood at a microphone shouting his jargon at innocent people going about their day. I would be annoyed if he was doing that in my town center, and have no issues asking him to pipe down. We voted, it's a democracy, end of remainers to suck it up and deal with it like adults please. YOU LOST go cry your tears quietly.

Chapter VII
Political Correctness and Brexorcism

Nigel Farage capitalised on the current obsession with political correctness to win the referendum. Granted, it is wrong to be offensive deliberately to disempower an individual or groups, but I sense that the movement for political correctness has now moved way past the point of a practical approach to improve our humanity. In some cases, it has been reduced to a set of personal preferences. Taken to extremes, it can restrict communication on important ideas and becomes the enemy of those issues which it seeks to address.

I noticed just how difficult this made life when trying to write satirical songs for the Remain movement and finding that we had a suite of "keyboard censors" on Facebook, trying to rewrite the songs via virtual committee. Having written a Chas & Dave inspired "Cockney Brexit Knees Up", I had numerous complaints about the use of the word tw..t. I had sampled "Eastenders" star Danny Dyer saying this about David Cameron. Apparently, it was OK for Dyer to say this on daytime TV, but not OK when sampled into the song as an "Eastender". OK, I thought, I'll change it to the very popular "Boll..cks to Brexit" refrain. I contacted Charlie Mullins OBE, CEO of Pimlico Plumbers and managed to get him to do a voiceover. However, I got just as many complaints, some due to the word and others due to the cheery nature of a Chas & Dave pastiche. I don't mind that people don't like a song. Once you have listened to a song thousands of times whilst recording it, I often never want to hear the song again myself. However, I must be honest, that sometimes I wonder if Remain want to win the fight against Brexit. Oh well, I went back to the drawing board ... in Chumbawumba terms "I get knocked down but I get up again."

Just recently I wrote a satirical "Country and Western Brexit Hoedown" called "Theresa May's a Remainer." There were no expletives in the song, so all was well, or so I thought. Alas, amidst the lyric was a reference to John Major taking about the Eurosceptics who he dubbed "basta..ds." I made a cheeky reference in the song with the phrase "Shoot the bastards, they're all insane." This was accompanied by a comedy gun shot and a horse "clip clopping" through the song. It could not be much more obvious that this was a piece of satirical comedy. Yet, even this received complaints from angry Daily Mail readers with a humour bypass operation and no sense of political history. No wonder Billy Bragg says that nobody makes protest songs any more …

Find the songs at www.academy-of-rock.bandcamp.com or via iTunes, Amazon etc. – Just Google "The Brexit Cowpokers" or the song titles. The lyrics to both songs are on the following pages so you may judge for yourselves the degree to which they offend, along with some of the angry quotes on "Theresa May's a Remainer" from the rabid Daily Maul readers.

Let's talk about BREX .. it

Theresa May's a Remainer :
A Country and Western Brexit Hoedown

Theresa May's a Remainer
May-be we should restrain-er
Stop Brexit luv, Don't abstain-er

No Deal is kind of insane-er
May's Deal is mostly Remain-er
Remain is a no-brainer

Grow a spine, Just don't complain
Stay in Europe, Let's just Remain
Shoot the bastards, They're all insane

Daily Mail complaints

Truth hurts wrote:

The words used in the song is unbelievable. He needs reporting. Clearly, someone that isn't mentally stable.

Cheerful in swale wrote:

Theres a better of the Gov getting the bill through Parliament in its current state before Christmas than this getting to number 1..or 2... or 3 in fact into the charts at all. What a terrible song and really do we need to use foul language in songs?

Kmuser1512 wrote:

Perhaps they were offended by the fact his song lyrics advocates violence & shooting political opponents?

Let's talk about BREX .. it

Boll..cks to Brexit :
A Chas & Dave Cockney Brexit Knees Up

Brexshit, Brexit, Brexshit, Brexit, Ave a banana

Well I've been goin' down the Brexit food bank for a while
While Jacob Rees-Mogg 'ee's dining out in style
The Banks are leaving Blighty and Dad's Army's on the streets
Whilst us poor buggers stay to fight on Brexit plates of meat

Eggs and Gammon, No Smoked Salmon, Traffic jammin', Bloody Spammin'

I'm really sick of Brexit, Why don't you fade away, I wanna find the exit, Please 'elp me Mrs May

Well I've bin' tryin' to score some drugs for my dia-betes
But I still can't buy no bog roll for me Brexit faeces
And I can't afford a crib in Maracheeses (fake Spanish town)
I might as well end it all in Bognor Regis

Diabetes, Mega faeces, Runny cheeses, Big diseases
Russian geezers, in "Bognor Reges", Lemon squeezers, Trump appeasers

I'm really sick of Brexit, Why don't you fade away, I wanna find the exit, Please 'elp me Mrs May

My wife's avin' a midlife Brexistential crisis
While me bruvver says I've joined Remainiac Isis
In football speak, Brexit was a quarter finalist
Theresa may need to see a Brexit psychiatrist

Customs Union, Big delusion, Is Arlene Foster even 'uman?
Barclays Bank, J. Arthur Rank, Aaron Banks, Sherman Tank
Soviet Union, Trump communion, Is this love or Brexit confusion?

I'm really sick of Brexit, Why don't you fade away, I wanna find the exit, Please 'elp me Mrs May

Chapter VIII
Money, Money, Money

I had a heated argument with a very young insurance man on the train who told me I'm an old man and I must get used to "his modern ways" re Brexit. I thought to myself that I will NEVER get used to his modern ways! I was close to another punching, but some other passengers came to my rescue ... as he shouted at me in his Brexit rage

Before this happened, my bicycle had set off a conversation with him. This man's basic claim was that no deal was project fear. He said that money would solve all problems for people on life saving drugs sourced from outside the UK. I pressed him with my knowledge of pharmaceuticals and asked him what he understood about supply chains and unlicensed medicines.

He said he did not understand anything about supply chains, but this did not matter. He added that people like Mark Carney were idiots. You might at this point say he was a waste of time to speak with, but there was quite an audience watching so I judged that he was not really my "subject". Some people appeared bemused at how little he knew but how confident he appeared to be about his ignorance. Here's a few things he said during the exchange:

"I haven't been to Continental Europe in decades, nor do I have the inclination to do so. A hard Brexit will not be the catastrophe the fear mongers are saying. Buyers will still buy and sellers will still sell, they'll just have to re-negotiate terms on a per case basis (old style) is all. Border security is paramount to slowing the Islamification of the nation. Many predict that Britain will become the manufacturing powerhouse of Europe while the other countries are left dealing with their unwanted and unforeseen immigration problems. I'm not saying Enoch Powell was right, but a lot of people seemed to have voted in favour of that ideology. The will of the people is what it is. 52 is more than 48 by 4%."

I decided that my best strategy was to let him make a fool of himself in front of his uninvited audience. For a young person, he was surprisingly unworldly, myopic and bitter.

Chapter IX
Yellow Vests

I make a point of visiting a local pub which is mostly frequented by leave voters. On one visit I am accosted by a chap who jokes about my hi-vis jacket, asking if I have come to read the meters. He knows a mutual friend who tells him that I write songs to help stop Brexit. It is the evening before the Vote Leave march and my subject is going to march the following morning. He warns me not to travel to London that day as he would definitely "have a go" if I'm seen there. I ignore this and ask him why he is marching. He has been drinking heavily and a stream of consciousness comes out. I listen patiently. The main points are:

He tells me the main problem with the country is that it is no longer Christian. I ask if he goes to church but he does not. He insists that he is a Christian and has indoctrinated his six children as Christians. He says the whole of the town is Muslim. I say that I don't see it. He says "maybe you need to open your eyes."

He tells me I'm a lefty as I say that I don't think the EU have caused all the problems he has explained to me. I'm certainly not a "lefty" but he does not listen so well and tells me I have a "lefty haircut". I'm not sure what that is but let it pass as it is in the way of my outcome.

Our mutual friend attempts to calm him down. I judge that no harm will come to me as he is the boyfriend of the landlord's daughter. He tells me that he will not go into kebab shops due to the filth that work there ... but he's not a "racialist".

He warns me not to go to London in the morning. I have no intention of adding to his numbers by proxy but I don't tell him that. We find that only a couple of thousand people show up ... Sometimes I worry that Remainers unwittingly boost the exposure of Vote Leave events by showing up for counter-protests. It is a vexed question with arguments on both sides ...

I am overall struck by the basket case of contradictions. Brexit has revealed the confusion of the human race ...

For those that are worried by the thought of civil unrest if we stop Brexit, here's a few facts to fight the perceptions:

1. This man did not punch me, although he was verbally aggressive and drunk.

2. The strategies we have discussed in Part I offer a suite of skills to defend yourself against the dark Brexit arts. If confrontation is not your preferred style find other ways to tune out of verbal aggression. NLP offers a suite of skills beyond this current book.

3. The Yellow Vests comprise about 13 people and a few keyboard warriors. They have always existed. They will be there whether we stay or leave the EU. However, if we leave, they will grow in confidence as their behaviour will have been legitimised by our Government.

4. In contrast, some 700 000 people protested peacefully at the People's march in 2018.

5. There is no legal mandate that requires us to leave the EU. The referendum was advisory despite what many people have been told. It is no more valid than an opinion poll.

6. The Yellow Vests are no more than an incidence of recency bias. This is when we assume that critical events are more frequent than they actually are, due to a recent occurrence.

Chapter X
The Immigrant Song

My wife Alison was minding her own business walking in Chatham High Street. She does not wear any anti-Brexit paraphernalia so is essentially invisible.

Without warning, a middle-aged man started talking to her. He was moaning about the "fact" that the local council had offered to take all the immigrants from London into the area (clearly not true).

Alison: "That's good."

Man: "But we're full."

Alison: "I'm an immigrant. I'm Irish."

Man: (realises he has been hoist by his own petard) "So am I." (He was from Liverpool but originally from Ireland too). "But there's still too many of them ..."

Alison: "If it's good enough for them, it's good enough for us?"

The man walked off up the road and then shouted back down the road "F..ck off."

Let's talk about BREX .. it

Chapter XI
Are you a Citizen of Nowhere?

Where Windrush Leads, Brexit Follows …

"In Limbo" is a poignant piece of music, inspired by the book of the same name, to highlight the desperate plight of EU Citizens left in uncertainty and fear for their futures, due to vacillation and abuse by our Government during the Brexit negotiations. Check out the In Limbo book for the full stories of tragedy, hope, hopelessness and hate which have characterised our DisUnited Kingdom since June 24 2016. In Limbo achieved number one status on Amazon, beating chart entries from Ed Sheeran, Abba and Kylie Minogue. This is remarkable for a song produced in a basement studio with no established artist as a brand. Even more remarkable is the back story of the song's production.

Due to advances in music technology I was able to gather voices from all over Europe and as far afield as Thailand to tell the tales of people's hopes, fears and experiences of being treated as "Citizens of Nowhere". Some facts:

IN LIMBO

FACT FILE

30 + EU Citizens on the song

Contributions from France, Germany, Ireland, Czech Republic, Hungary, Poland, Greece, Spain, Italy, The Netherlands

132 + tracks to mix !!!

3 months in the making

Let's talk about BREX .. it

In Limbo was conceived as a downbeat groove in my studio with a major lift via a chorus delivered by professional singer Rachel Ashley and a supremely great animated film from Mark Duffy. Comparisons have been made with Moby, Leftfield, Pink Floyd and Prince.

Whilst we aimed to achieve UK top 40 chart success with the song, this was not the main ambition. I detected a need to mainstream the issues of the EU Citizens in UK and UK Ex Pats in Europe via our populist media. Ultimately the song did not reach the chart due to the fragmentation of the Remain movement and some distaste of our populist media by Remainers. As a result, we did not cut through to the Brexiteer's thought space. I found that I was relatively alone in thinking that we needed to break outside of Remain bubbles, nonetheless it was still a great achievement by all that contributed.

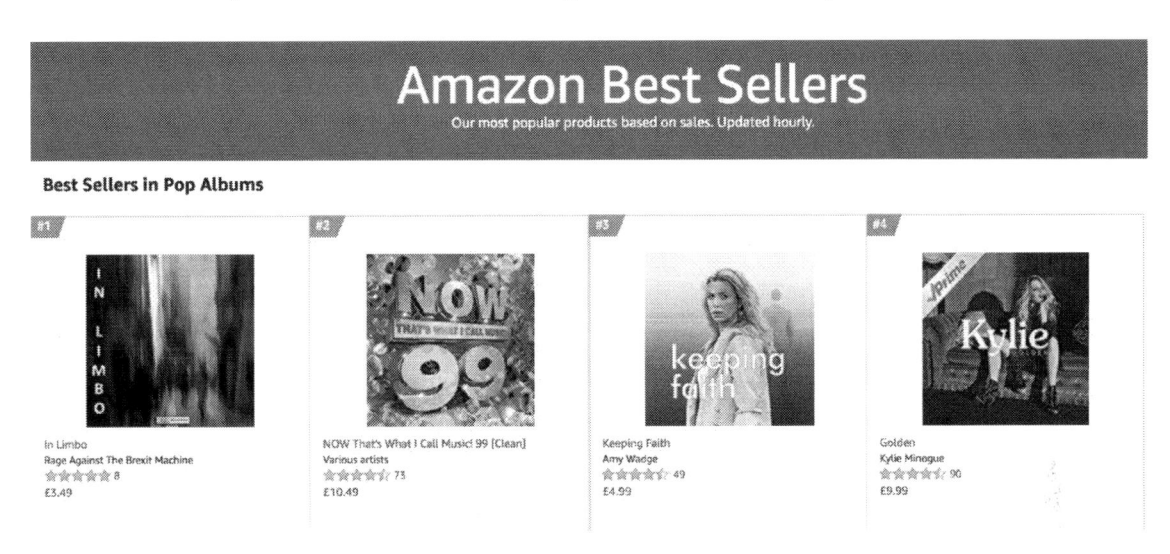

Amazon Best Sellers
Our most popular products based on sales. Updated hourly.

Best Sellers in Pop Albums

#1	#2	#3	#4
In Limbo Rage Against The Brexit Machine ★★★★★ 8 £3.49	NOW That's What I Call Music! 99 [Clean] Various artists ★★★★½ 73 £10.49	Keeping Faith Amy Wadge ★★★★½ 49 £4.99	Golden Kylie Minogue ★★★★½ 90 £9.99

Our Government continues to use EU Citizens as bargaining chips in their desperate attempts to negotiate a "Cake and Eat it Brexit deal". Yet, nearly three years have passed and we still have no clarity about the future for **all people** living in UK.

I have heard stories of people who were threatened with being burned alive by our so-called tolerant British people. When I make comparisons with the emergence of Nazi Germany, I am often told that this is offensive. Well, it is offensive to be threatened to be burned alive and if the truth hurts in our sanitised society, then so be it. I am too old to worry about political correctness … if you are bored by Brexit, frankly, so am I and I make no apology at continuing to make the argument against it. It is even written in the snow …

Let's talk about BREX .. it

We noted that music is the language of the emotions earlier. The 2016 referendum was won by a naked appeal to the emotions of the people when Nigel Farage asked people to vote with their hearts (bypassing their heads). Whether you like or loathe Nigel, his strategy surprised nearly everyone, including himself, but not Cambridge Analytica …

However, it does not do to copy a strategy. Rather we must better it …

There is a long legacy of protest through music, from Nina Simone, Pete Seeger, through Joan Baez, Tracey Chapman, John Lennon, Prince, Marvin Gaye, Kate Bush and Billy Bragg et al. However, nobody has so far rewritten Lennon's classic "Give Brexit a Chance", as Brexit has already been given some two years and the indicators are that Brexit has indeed made peace a less likely result of the civil war that is ripping families, industries and communities apart in Britain.

Let's talk about BREX .. it

Here is the hall of fame from the In Limbo track:

Lead vocals: Rachel Ashley

Bass and ambient bass textures: Jason Bell

A mystery soprano opera singer

Animated film production: Mark Duffy

Violin ambience: Kristina Howells

In Limbo spoken word testimonies and choir members: Erwin Schaefer, Sian Davies, Anette Pollner, Sabine Dor, Veronika V, Vicky Tessio, Malgorzata Piotrowska, Agnes Pinteaux, Emma Pinteaux, Lily Pinteaux, Maria Llorente, Rohan Nair, Peter De Clerq, Susanna Leissle, Lotti Newstead, Christina Howells, Xavier Kreiss, Silvia Impellizeri, Lisa Lanfranchi, Veronique Martin.

Cover art: Allisdhair McNaull

Let's talk about BREX .. it

Citizens of Nowhere

Where Windrush Leads Brexit Follows ...

Find "In Limbo" on iTunes, Amazon and YouTube etc.

Google "In Limbo, Voices for Europe."

Check the book of the same name out.

Chapter XII
Trumptown and Brexit

Where Brexit leads, Trump follows ... Our Brexit referendum precedes the election of Donald Trump by six months or so. In conversation with my US friends, I note that many of the same effects we experienced over here were echoed in America, albeit with a six-month time delay. For example, triumphalism, a string of legal challenges and so on.

One important difference is that, like dogs, Brexit is not just for Christmas, it's for life. Brexit is a constitutional change that will be life changing. After five years, Trump may be gone etc. Just why do people vote for a guy that shuts the Government down and suspends everyone's wages if he does not get his own way? Just imagine this happening in normal life?

The phenomenon of Trump is a parallel universe with Brexit. Whatever your feelings about Trump, you cannot deny that he has seized the hearts and minds of much of the population of America, particularly those who enjoy soundbites and who feel left behind by modern life. Therefore, there are some important if unpalatable lessons inherent in a study of Trump:

1. In a complex world, the person(s) who can simplify complexity into 3 or 4 words stands to control the minds of the masses, regardless of the merits of the truth.

2. In a post-truth world, some people actually admire people who openly admit to lying. It is considered a badge of honour by people who are dispossessed by the establishment.

3. In a populist world, people who stand up to the establishment are applauded by the masses, regardless of their own motives in doing so.

We have a choice: To copy these designs or better them. We must be brief, honest and reach people who feel left behind, if we are to beat the populists at their own game.

Let's talk about BREX .. it

We finish this segue with the lyrics to our song Trumptown, an acid jazz song inspired by the lyrical genius of Ian Dury and the childlike nursery rhymes of Syd Barrett.

Trumptown

Trump built a wall
Mexicans fall
He's 10 feet tall
Our skins they crawl

He's no Baptist
Nor a trappist
A neo-fascist
Ashes to ashes

Trump had a windfall
Left with bugger all
Trump had a brawl
The press had a ball

He's no Baptist
A neo-fascist

Find Trumptown on iTunes, Amazon and YouTube etc.

Google "Trumptown, The Trumpeteers"

Let's talk about BREX .. it

Chapter XIII
Tennis Elbowed

I had just finished delivering a leadership master class at a local tennis club and was about to pack my car up with the equipment. Strangely my work involves taking musical instruments such as guitars and amplifiers to business events, see www.academy-of-rock.co.uk Some people had wanted to meet me afterwards for a cup of coffee so I decided to leave my guitars at the reception desk. I had two Fender Stratocasters with me, both of them proudly displaying "Boll..cks to Brexit stickers" and I asked the receptionist if it would be alright to leave them at reception behind the desk and out of sight. The receptionist agreed and joked if she could play the guitar whilst I drank coffee. It was an amusing and genial brief encounter.

A few minutes later the conference manager came over to me and said: " I'm afraid you will have to take the guitars away from the reception desk as they are likely to cause offence to staff". My guitars are lying flat on a table behind reception. I'd say that they were totally invisible to staff and customers. I'd taken some care to put them in the best place, giving consideration to the club's client base. I'm doing a little bit of mind reading here but I'd say that what she meant was that she was offended by the stickers on them, but had not the courage to say so.

I ask her what the problem is. She appears not to be able to explain it to me, so I enquire (loudly):

"So is it the Boll..cks that is offensive or the Brexit?"

I point out that Brexit is far more offensive ...

She does not really know what is offensive about the guitars ... But she insists I move the guitars. So, I move them into the public area where guests are all drinking tea etc. and point this out to her. She has made an invisible problem more visible. She does not know what to do or say.

As a result, I am unable recommend Avenue Tennis to 48% of the British population. And they say that Remainers are snowflakes ... WTF ???

Let's talk about BREX .. it

Offensive guitars ...

Chapter XIV
A Fisherman's tail

I met the Faversham Fisherman, Mark, at the Boll..cks to Brexit bus protest. It turns out that Mark is a real character. Quite charming and with many a "fisherman's tale" to tell. He was a participant in Nigel Farage's Fish protest versus Bob Geldof. Mark had even written a song about Bob, who lives in the same town.

Mark was drawn by my guitar as he loved music. Others who knew him well from the town had managed to avoid him, but I enjoy talking so I listened for one hour in mostly non-directive and autonomous and co-operative mode from John Heron's model. The main points of that conversation are recorded here.

We began by me admitting my relative lack of knowledge about fishing. I made one point, that I felt someone must make rules about catching fish, otherwise we would catch all the fish from the oceans. That duty currently fell to the EU. I then invited him to fill in my knowledge gaps. Mark agreed that rules were needed but felt that the fishermen could self-regulate. I am doubtful due to the human condition of moral hazard, but I say nothing. We move on.

Mark's essential point is that he cannot make a good living from the quotas of fish that he is allowed to catch. In common with around 80% of British fisherman he operates from a small boat. He can catch his entire quota in one day. Quotas disproportionately disadvantage smaller boats and I understand his angst. European boats tend to be bigger and I was left wondering whether our own Government had somehow left our fishing industry behind.

The basic economics are that he can only fish on one day per week, the diesel to run his boat is quite expensive and it is barely worth the effort to continue.

I asked him about leaving the EU. If we left, would he be much better off, a little better off, the same or worse off. It seemed as though he'd not given this much thought. After a long pause, he said he would be a little better off but not massively. This was a surprise to me (and him, I sense).

Let's talk about BREX .. it

Having listened for some 45 minutes, I offered a small insight. I said that I was mainly worried about my kids. We had not discussed families, but it prompted him to tell me that he had a daughter. I asked:

"Does your daughter plan to follow you into the business?"

"No", he answered, "she likes horses."

I left the conversation there. I then asked Mark to perform his Bob Geldof song in the square which he did. It was very funny, even though it was clear that he could not stand Bob. A few Remainers winced as I encouraged him to have his voice heard.

A few hours later, Mark turned up to greet the Boll..cks to Brexit bus. He had been home to retrieve a CD of protest songs for me, written by relatives of Pete Seeger. He had also been to the pub and donned an equally offensive Brexit fisherman's T-shirt. He was ready to perform his song again, so I recommended he speak with Madeleina Kay who was leading the charge on the protest. Apparently, he was refused.

I was told afterwards that Mark was an EDL supporter, which is why nobody would talk to him. He came across as charming. But then again, so does Nigel Farage …

Mark clearly constitutes one of the people "left behind" by our Government. We may not all want to share our homes with such people, but we ignore them at our peril …

Chapter XV
Let's write about Brexit

One of the more practical ways of resisting Brexit is to write a letter. We are told that letters should be polite, courteous and ask questions to prick the conscience of the people we write to. Many people believe that MPs read long letters and there are plenty of examples of good letters you can find online to make your point. I have largely chosen to write more pointed letters, as these examples demonstrate. You may disagree with the satirical or even acidic style, but sometimes a short punchy letter makes a point more forcefully than an essay. Your choice of course.

Securing support

This is my letter to Sir Richard Branson which secured his endorsement of Gina Miller's project. A relatively simple matter.

Hello nnn,

Not sure if you have been watching our circus formerly known as Brexit, but I had a contact from Gina Miller, the woman who single-handedly overturned Theresa May's idea that she could sidestep Parliament on the matter, and who faced threats of gang rape and beheading because of her principled stand for justice.

She is planning further action, but time is of the essence and wonders if you might pass her phone number on to Richard.

If Richard is happy to chat Gina's mobile is 0044 xxxx xxxxxx

All the best and speak soon

Peter

Let's talk about BREX .. it

Letters to Parliament

Theresa,

Further to my previous letter, I have been told that I was "too generous" in my requests for backing Brexit. I have now been in consultations with David Davis and would add the following items to the "rider":

- Knighthoods for ALL who back Brexit.

- 200 Tonnes of Bovril available in local cafés.

- A lifetime's supply of Chocolate buttons and Imperial Leather.

- Reinstatement of Watney's Red Barrel in all pubs and removal of all foreign beers and Prosecco.

- Reintroduction of bear-baiting, syphilis and plague as national pastimes and international diseases.

- Remaking The X Factor as The eXecution Factor, a game show where benefit scroungers compete for the "ultimate prize" of hanging.

Remember, "nothing is agreed until everything is agreed."

p.s. I predict that at least half and probably a lot more than half of the people are now very angry and will not take this lying down. I urge you to begin with the Chocolate buttons and the Imperial Leather.

Wham Bam, TY Ma'am

Peter Cook

The Media

In other cases, it is true that politicians are just as susceptible as us in reading letters to newspapers and even gossip columns. To get a letter into a national newspaper absolutely demands brevity, currency and some unique element. Here are a few that have worked over the ages:

My letter from Nigel Farage

I wrote to my MEP Nigel Farage requesting a financial assessment of the benefits of Brexit.

I was expecting a mathematical answer but was astonished to receive a reply blaming those bloody Greek philosophers Plato and Aristotle:

"May I suggest some general reading for you: Hobbes, Locke, Von Mises, Hayek, Fukuyama. The EU is based on the philosophy of Plato rather than Aristotle – that's why continental Europe keeps descending into tyranny whilst the UK escapes – we have done so again in Brexit and the EU's tyranny is for example exposed in Greece.

"Democracy is the real Brexit prize and from it flows a stable political system, the rule of law and sustained economic prosperity. Change of course always involves some disruption, and there is a short-term cost to that, but the long-term gains from the above are priceless. The mistake was joining the EU project in the first place – that is where responsibility for the costs involved in leaving should fall."

Who knew that philosophers were to blame for our current business uncertainties? I imagine Mick Jagger would have said "you Kant always get what you want".

Peter Cook, Kent

Once the subway rush passes, the band heads to 10 Downing Street and plants itself in front of Theresa May's office to play her favorite song, "Dancing Queen," from Abba. Peter Cook knows he annoys the head of the government but does not give up. He wants to convey two messages: consider the possibility of a new vote and we are closely monitoring the negotiations with Brussels and the false promises of Brexit.

> *"Theresa May was greeting the Commonwealth leaders in April, we stood on the path of the procession to get our message across, she always had a tough message against immigration, but when she wants to negotiate a free trade agreement, exchange with India or Pakistan, will not they ask for the free movement of people as well as goods? What will Brexit have brought to us? I want her to recognize it and to tell people."*

For Theresa May to understand that opponents of Brexit, who have probably missed the referendum campaign, will no longer be silent, the consultant sang the song Police: "Every step you take, I'll be watching you" (' I'll watch every step of yours, "he hums, laughing. He tells :

> *She glared at me, I would have dreamed that she did like Emmanuel Macron, that she came to discuss, to debate with me, she would have shown that she knows how to negotiate, that she can surprise the other party, disarm it. "*

But no !

Article for Premiere French magazine L'Obs

Chapter XVI
Spooking out your MP

Writing letters is one thing. Stalking out your MP at public or private meetings quite another. My MP is Rehman Chishti, a nice enough chap who succeeds mostly by avoiding his electorate in the safe seat of Rainham in Kent. Formerly a Labour candidate, Rehman had a religious conversion some time ago, presumably as there was a better career to be had as a Conservative in the post Dockyard era. He has consistently voted with the PM of the day and as a result became Party Vice Chair for Communities a while back. I went to the same school as him for a couple of years where he also followed the rules and became a prefect. Sadly, I did not and that accounts for my entire life in working with the establishment, but we all have our crosses to bear.

Life has not been so kind to Mr Chishti of late. He was implicated in taking consultancy fees of £200 per hour from a Saudi Think Tank just recently. Needless to say there are quite a few people who feel that justice should also be metered out for his tendency to ignore his constituents. One of them contacted me after my assault by Brexiteers, a fellow Remainer and, who it seemed had a long track record of trying to get Mr Chishti to serve his constituents.

This is one of those "you had to be here" moments but I will try to explain longhand in this story … it is in two parts and I've saved the best till last so read on …

PART I – Don't Stand So Close To Me

I had the immense pleasure of going down to my local Council surgery to speak with the local councillor recently at the request of a mystery Remain voter who dislikes feckless politicians. His intention was to use me as a "Trojan Horse" to put another nail in Rehman Chishti's coffin. This followed Rehman's resignation from his position in the Conservative Party.

On arrival, we were met by the Councillor for Rainham North, Martin Potter. Martin became fixated on my "F…CK BREXIT" T-Shirt as he opened the door to his office. Caught like a rabbit in headlights, he seemed unable to let us into his surgery, burbling and stuttering, as he attempted to articulate his problem with the T-Shirt at the door … he hesitated endlessly …

Martin: "Erm, I cannot speak with you with that T-Shirt on."

Me: "What is troubling you? We came to speak with you about a local policing issue."

Martin: "It's the T-Shirt – I cannot speak with you with that word."

Me: "What, Brexit?"

Him: "Erm, no …" dithering and fumbling nervously.

Me (very loudly so that front desk person could hear): "Oh, you mean F…CK. I think you will find much worse out there in Chatham High Street."

Him: "It's just I cannot speak with you with that word on the shirt …"

Me: "Well, to be honest I find your green Lacoste T-Shirt unbearably boring, but I'm not going to mention it. Now, we don't have the BBC filming here. We are not recording this. We are on our own in your office. What is your problem really" … (no answer) … later on … "Would you like me to take my top off?"

Him: "That would help."

Fortunately for everyone I did have two tops on … !!! So, I removed the T-Shirt.

Footnote … Martin kept mentioning the T-Shirt throughout the meeting, even though I no longer had it on. Two days later, it was still the main subject of his e-mail response to me. I imagine he has had to receive therapy for this by now …

Dear Peter,

Thank you for visiting my surgery on Saturday, and for removing the t-shirt with the offensive f**k word on it so we could engage in dialogue on reasonable terms.

I was very sorry to hear of the incident on the train in Gillingham, and I do hope my advice regarding the Office of Police Conduct yields a full and proper investigation into what went wrong with the police response. As requested, I have also copied Mr Chishti's office into this email and included the contact details below:

Email: Rehman.Chishti.mp@parliament.uk

Tel: 01634 570118

Best regards
Martin

Let's talk about BREX .. it

Eventually, after further nervous hesitation, we entered his office and got down to business. Martin is still completely phased by our initial conversation and keeps referring to it, despite my ignoring it. He agrees to getting a meeting with Rehman Chishti to discuss the failure of the Police after I explain that I understand Mr Chishti really cares about local issues, although he allegedly spends an awful lot of time assisting Saudi Arabia with advice ... He looks terrified as he continues to think about the T-Shirt ...

PART II – Close Encounters with Rehman Chishti

Eventually we leave, happy with the outcome (although he has not contacted me since, true to form). I have enjoyed the brief encounter with my mystery friend so I ask if he would like a cup of tea. We turn the corner to the café in the precinct. As we walk in, who should be there but the MP Rehman Chishti himself !!! ... My friend announces our arrival and begins to introduce me to Rehman ...

"May I introduce you to ... "

Rehman (interrupting): "Peter Cook" ... somehow he knows me!!

Me: "Oh, we've never met. I'm not the dead comedian."

Rehman: "I know who you are. You were very rude to me on Twitter."

Me: "I wasn't. I wrote you some letters, but you don't ever answer them."

Rehman: "My Parliamentary record shows I always answer every letter" (... still living the dream as a prefect at school).

Me: "You do answer the letters, but you don't actually ever answer the questions. They are vague generalisations or nominalisations in NLP speak. Or, if you prefer, cut and paste."

Rehman: "I personalise all my letters."

Me: "OK, you put Dear Peter at the top. We did not come in here to talk about that, so enjoy your coffee"

Rehman: "You called me a turd on Twitter."

Me: "Actually I don't think I called you a TURD, I think it was a TWAT but they both start with a T" (emphasising the words turd and twat – the café was full and people started listening. They will have known who Rehman Chishti was).

Me: "I'm from Gillingham. Although I have three degrees, I'm told I have a "Labour accent. My wife says I'm intelligent scum ..."

Rehman: "So am I from Gillingham. I'd not go so far as your wife."

Me: "But she knows me and, it's true I am intelligent scum. We both went to the same school."

Rehman: "The point is that this sort of language is not for Twitter."

Me: "I disagree. If you go down to Chatham, you will find words such as TURD and TWAT are the currency of people in Medway. The vernacular of Chatham is the same as Twitter. I always try to settle issues by personal and private communications. When I don't get any answers, I take the debate outside into the public domain and use direct language as it gets to the heart of the matter. I think you should get outside more in the area. Anyway, I came to speak about another matter (explains what we had done).

We ended up agreeing to meet to discuss police matter. I promised not to mention turds twats, Brexit and Saudi arms trade in our subsequent meeting.

We shook hands. He still had a coffee with some mystery guy. Having sat down for 30 seconds or so, they both left the café, leaving their coffees behind. I'm not sure who the other guy was, but I had a distinct feeling that they did not want us listening in ... ☺

Lessons Learned

A direct approach can be more effective than all the e-mails and tweets.

An unusual artefact can help "announce' you. However, beware of gimmicks per se as they wear out. But symbolism can cut through words in quite remarkable ways.

A plan for such encounters matters and also the ability to be spontaneous.

Rehman Chishti tried to invoke position power at the beginning of our meeting. I did not accept this attempt to introduce hierarchy.

Brexit Reflections

Chapter XVII
An Unhealthy Brexit

Brexit has caused many of us to examine out values and motives and to that extent it is a good thing. The chaotic twists and turns in Government have increased the likelihood of a chaotic no deal Brexit, threatening food supplies, fuel and continuity of supply for medicines. I have been working to help Wendy Nowak, a diabetic who relies on insulin and other medication for her survival. Wendy has spearheaded a campaign called "Who Cares About Brexit" (www.brexitrage.com) to highlight the healthcare and medicine shortage problems that a No Deal Brexit will cause should our Government continue to count the clock down to April Fools' Brexit day and then have an "accidental Brexit". People often ask why I care about Brexit, and here I offer some personal reflections.

Being happy and healthy

Firstly, I am very lucky in so far that I don't currently have any medical conditions so there is no self interest in my reason to set this project up … My self-interest goes right back to being 11 years old. At the age of five, I wanted to be in The Beatles … sadly all the jobs were taken, even the drummer's position! I came from a poor background and my parents "let me be" as the last child of six … I was something of a surprise as my Mum was 45 and Dad 67 on arrival and she claimed I was a Virgin birth … My Mum had more or less guided the other children into safe and steady jobs such as the army and engineering, but I recall her saying later on that "I was different" … so I passed the 11 + exams and went to Gillingham Grammar School, where David Frost had attended. I was far from the best student. However, I was encouraged to gravitate towards what I loved. That was science for the most part … especially Chemistry. I used to read ahead of the subject and was bullied for being the best Chemistry student. The old Chemistry teacher, a hoary old weasel from Yorkshire called Mr Harrison, when asking questions, would always say "Don't tell 'em Cook" before letting the class attempt answers!

I realised almost immediately that I wanted to be a scientist. Eventually I left the school at 18, having decided not to go to University and applied for two jobs and was accepted for both. I had a gruelling day long interview with Shell and later on a much more chaotic one at The Wellcome Foundation (they had forgotten I was coming).

A No-Tears Brexit

On the occasion of taking my mother in law to the hospital for her final journey, we got talking with the Ambulance driver whilst waiting in the "Resuss" department. She had observed my T-Shirt and was initially guarded as she was not sure if I was a Brexiteer. Once it became obvious that I was not, a wave of relief came over her. She first told me that they were very careful about picking people up from my area as they were often "Old Age Brexiteers" and, of course I fitted the profile, age wise!

She went on to say that one day her 13-year-old daughter was crying and when she asked why it was because of Brexit and her concerns about the future.

Another example from a 14-year-old daughter talking about her mum illustrates the need for a "No-Death Brexit." Will our Government sign off on this?

"My mum has asthma, diabetes and a rare auto immune condition. Her drugs come from Italy, Ireland and Germany. She has Livedoid Vasculopathy and takes Rivaroxaban, a new drug made in the EU. It stops her blood clotting and is safer than Warfarin.

A No Deal Brexit will put her life at risk. She may lose her legs without continuity of medication. Our Government's glib statements about stockpiling ignore border delays and other logistics problems. They are playing fast and loose with people's lives."

I accepted the latter, in part because one of the interviewers told me that the Wellcome club had the longest bar in Dartford, but mostly because I kind of liked the quaint ethos of a company that made a profit and used that money to heal the world. Wellcome was perhaps the World's only philanthropic pharmaceutical company ...

Anyway, I was given the great privilege to develop ground-breaking treatments for diabetes, herpes and the first HIV / AIDS drug. My best school friend had contracted HIV whilst enjoying himself too much in California. Never before had I had a job that married my passions with a purpose. My choice, to get a job and follow up part time with three degrees, was, in hindsight, a wise one. Does this give me a few chips on my shoulders about my level of intelligence in comparison to our Government? Well, yes, it does.

We worked like Trojans and played in the same spirit. But always the work came before the play, an ethos which I have carried forward to this day, to the delight of my clients and the irritation of a few people through my razor-sharp focus and insistence on doing things properly ... oh well ...

When nostalgia is a dangerous thing

This leads me to my point. I do not intend to see our Government throw away all that advancement in science and innovation to take us back to the 1950's, all for the sake of some romantic notions of getting a country back we never lost, a 50 pence souvenir and a blue passport. In 1800, our life expectancy in the UK was around 40 years. Advances in medicine have been a major contribution to our ability to live longer, healthier and happier lives, along with several other improvements in surgery, disinfection and nutrition etc. We mostly take these benefits for granted until they are lost. In the words of Joni Mitchell:

"Don't it always seem to go?

That you don't know what you've got till it's gone"

Ignoramuses such as Jacob Rees-Mogg may be able to say a few long words and quote Latin in the House of Commons to create a sense of deference with the masses, but Mogg, Boris, Duncan Smith et al have no f..cking clue about the building blocks of what we have achieved as a nation. I also have Latin and Ancient Greek O' Levels, so Mogg can f..ck off ... excuse my Latin ...

"Mortem Parca affert, opes rursus ac facultates aufert ..."

Let's talk about BREX .. it

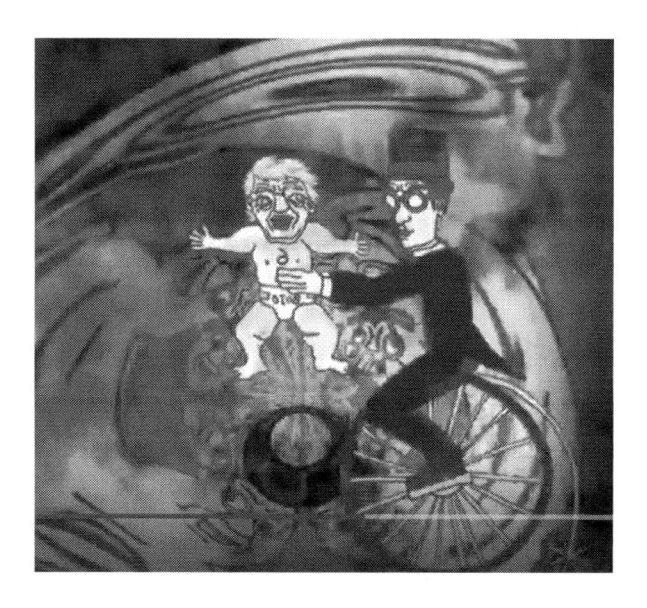

Jacob Rees-Mogg swaddles the baby Boris ...

People have no idea what we are throwing away and the consequences of doing so. UK Health Minister Matt Hancock said that he could not guarantee medicine supplies in the event of a No Deal Brexit. In a confusing series of messages Hancock has told pharma companies to stockpile drugs. Then he told the patients to do it, after it became apparent that pharmacies did not have capacity. Recently he has told pharmacies not to stockpile or allow patients to do so, as it may create shortages. Oh, yes, and the Government have bought a few fridges. In some cases, drug stability and storage requirements make it impossible to enact these strategies in any case. In any case, patients with orphan conditions or on unlicensed medicines will find it very difficult to source their medication.

Please wake up and think a little about the people you know that rely on medication for their continuing existence rather than your own circumstances and what's on Strictly. All progress relies on unreasonable people and I have been privileged to work with a good bunch of them over the years. It has also made me what a few consider "unreasonable", expecting better when others accept mediocre.

Why Do You Care? Please share your stories via Wendy's Facebook page.

Let's talk about BREX .. it

No Deal Brexit Reflection

From a friend ...

I'm at the stage of hoping Brexit happens. I'm looking forward to seeing the arses that voted for this being made redundant, finding no food in the shops, no help when their granny needs social services, discovering that Britain isn't a superpower anymore and that no ... the WTO won't just send us everything we want for less than we paid the EU countries. I'm going to enjoy seeing these twazzocks in pain ... especially when they try to get hospital treatment and there are too few staff to see them let alone treat them ...

oh but of course ... Nigel Farage has just told us we should get rid of the NHS and have an insurance-based health system ... so you won't get more than a paracetamol if you can't afford the best policy... welcome to the Banana Republic of England .... because Scotland, Wales and Northern Ireland will all leave this mad, despotic UK ... mainly because they are not even permitted a voice with this insane Tory government ... welcome to Brexit ...

Thanks to Carol Norwell

Chapter XVIII
The Smiths

I had a great conversation about Brexit with a woman who does not vote nor read newspapers in W.H. Smith today. She will vote against Brexit in any future election or vote. The lack of awareness was staggering, but at least she was pleased to have an intelligent dialogue. We were there for ages though. The conversation started after she saw my "Break Brexit Before Brexit Breaks Britain" T-Shirt.

And complimented for my skills and patience by the young shop assistant who was earwigging in on the conversation with the customer. And I only went in to hide copies of The Daily Mail, Express and The Sun!

Three in one. The T-Shirt is the conversation starter although other things work ... My main asset in the conversation was not judging her astonishingly low levels of knowledge about Brexit and respecting her candour in saying she did not vote.

Let's talk about BREX .. it

Chapter XIX
Late night, Maudlin Street

Coming out of my home train station in Kent last night at 12.30 was instructive ... with two OABs (Old Age Brexiteers) - a large man with shopping basket on wheels and his wife ... we were confined in the lift ... lucky nobody farted!

HIM: "I'm f..cked, let's get a taxi home. I can't walk anymore."

I smile knowingly and they gaze at me and my bicycle.

HIM: (looking at bicycle) "Boll..cks to Brexit, yeah Boll..cks to Brexit." .. (starts almost singing it to himself)

ME: "Yes, Boll..cks to Brexit. It's a pile of shite." (they nod).

All get out of lift. They are waddling in front of me and in my way, but no spatial skills. I manage to pass them and get on my way ... he is still muttering Boll..cks to Brexit to his wife ...

I overhear him telling his wife: "Yeah, I fought the Pakis in the 80's ... and I fought the Chinkies ... That EU ... load of wan...ers." ... yada yada

ME: "I really don't think you understand anything about Brexit."

They look at me, puzzled. I cycle off ... I mean, really, what's the point? I'm tired and I assess this as a no-win situation.

I comfort myself with the thought that they are probably not long for this world given their overall state of health ... Bad boy Peter for thinking this!

Later on, I am greeted at the local Turkish veg shop by a resounding burst of "Boll..cks to Brexit" from the shop assistant ☺ I have "trained" them over several months and am now greeted with this. At least they understand it better than the natives!

The interesting reflection is that my use of a catchphrase slipped into the man's consciousness without questioning the meaning. I've observed this many times. Sometimes Remainers gold-plate their methods for Brexorcism when "simple" often reaches the parts that "complex" does not ...

BREAK BREXIT
BEFORE BREXIT
BREAKS BRITAIN
www.brexitrage.com
BOLLOCKS TO BREXIT!!
People's Vote
Demand a vote on the Brexit deal
9028
08

Chapter XX
Brief Encounters of the 3rd kind

Brexorcisms don't have to take hours. Sometimes a brief encounter is worthwhile as opportunities present themselves, as these examples demonstrate:

I met a 40-year-old woman at a coffee shop opposite Marylebone station. After a brief conversation, she told me she did not vote. After I pointed out that my life was over, but her life mattered re Brexit, she agreed that oblivion was not an overall helpful place. This was surprisingly simple and quick. I suspect she just needed pushing over the line towards caring more.

A North London leaver with seven friends at the same café, who initially joked that he was pleased he did not have to punch me as I'd already been done! ☺ A good icebreaker. He was subsequently shocked when I showed him the actual pictures of me being punched. It had not seemed real in casual conversation. I'm not sure he even believed me as I joked about it during the "rapport" building stage. This made him think about the hostile environment we have invited in via Brexit.

A genial conversation ensued. He was pleasantly surprised to meet a Remainer that did not lecture him. No Brexorcism was achieved with him of course but his friends were all giving my bicycle the thumbs up by the time I left. He gave the familiar argument that his dad fought in the war and that came out well, so Brexit would be OK ... I chose to let it be, having mentioned that there were some differences between a war with a common enemy and a desperate situation versus our current situation of a divided nation and a self-induced crisis. We had a cordial exchange on this, and both listened well.

Having boarded the train, I met an old age pensioner with his kids and grandchildren on Chiltern Trains going to Wembley. He initiated a long chat with me about how we can turn the minds of politicians, after he spotted the hoarding on my bicycle. This was the catalyst to the conversation which otherwise would not have happened.

Later on, an old woman glared endlessly at the sign whilst waiting to get off further up the line at Ruislip - I could not make eye contact so I said "sorry" to break her fixed gaze at the sign, thinking her to be a Brexiteer. She then told me she voted to join the EU in

1975, voted Remain in 2016 and was delighted to see people still fighting to stay in Europe. She was almost in tears as she left the train. A heart-warming moment.

On my return journey, I received numerous nervous smiles at Victoria and Marylebone stations ... and a bit of glaring at Victoria ... It's strange how the River Thames seems to be a tipping point for glaring ☺

I returned with the football supporters from Wembley ... I don't know what teams they supported but I thought that this might have led to trouble and was slightly cautious as I did not wish to be punched again. However, all were OK ... mostly amused smiles and a bit of glaring at the sign ... I guess their team must have won ....

Finally, the station attendant at Orpington stood staring at the bicycle sign. I wondered why and eventually made eye contact. He broke out in a broad smile. He then went to get his colleagues to look at the bicycle and could not believe I'd been punched for wearing a T-shirt ...

Chapter XXI
To the Brexit Manor Born

Brexit conversations happen in the strangest places. Whilst at Hever Castle in Kent we were looking at the medieval instruments of torture. I joked to my son's guest from overseas that our far-right politician Jacob Rees-Mogg probably had these instruments in his bedroom. This was the direction of travel if Brexit happened.

An indignant country gent intervened, saying that my comment was ignorant as he scuttled off down the medieval stairs. A brief exchange ensured, which could be summarised as:

"You cad"

"You bounder"

"You are a traitor to the state sir"

"Come outside and say that by the moat"

The curator fidgeted uncomfortably, wondering where this might lead.

It was a pity I did not have my Ikea Ducking Stool handy …

I note that most English people simply scowl when confronted by a T-Shirt or a conversation such as this. It will be our undoing …

PART III

Defence Against the Dark Brexit Arts

Defence Against the Dark Brexit Arts

In this section I've produced a compendium of commonly asked questions or statements that Brexiteers ask or make about Brexit. There are no magic bullet answers to such challenges since:

- The Brexiteer may not be awake, alert or receptive. See our thoughts on waking up your subjects in Part II.

- Only 7% of the overall communication is down to the syntax. So, snappy responses are one thing, but getting people to understand and accept those answers usually requires much harder work on the preparatory phase. See our thoughts on warming up your subjects. Remember all is different online when compared with real life, when you are mostly working only with the 7% plus the odd meme and video. This is not communication. It is transmission. It may also be asynchronous and or fragmented by distance and time.

- Context / warm up is everything. You may well need a bank balance of credit in order to slay a "sacred Brexit cow" or gammon.

- And a host of other issues may prevent successful two-way communications.

Nonetheless I've attempted to list some general lines of attack in the hope that it will help "arm" you with ways to "challenge people without tears."

Remember that you can challenge people in both directive and non-directive ways. Use the full spectrum of John Heron's model for maximum impact on your subject. You will mostly be working in collaborative and autonomous mode unless you are an acknowledged expert. Even then that expertise may not be accepted by your subject.

Let's talk about BREX .. it

Brexit Apathy

Typically, Brexiteers say things like:

> "Let's get it over and done with."
>
> "Just want to get out."
>
> "Leave means Leave."
>
> "Just get out and be done with it as that what we voted for."
>
> "I'm really sick of Brexit."

Suitable challenges begin with the following arguments:

I'm sick of Brexit. What do you think we have got after nearly three years of negotiations?

What did you vote for? Later on ... To what extent have you gotten this?

Imperialism

Typical objections I have heard leave voters use include mantras such as:

> "They (EU) need us more than we need them."
>
> "The EU need our money. We should threaten not to pay."
>
> "If they ask for the £39 million, we should just bomb France."
>
> "Why should we pay any money anyway?"
>
> "All PM May needs to do is to play these EU gangsters at their own game. Simply tell them OK. No problem if you don't want to help. I'll just go back to the UK and organise another referendum with just the two options on the ballot for the people to choose from. My deal. Leave with NO £40 Billion and onto WTO rules Just the thought of the British people having the power to tell the EU where to go with its £40

Let's talk about BREX .. it

BILLION ransom demand would terrify them all in Brussels because they know full well that given the options above which they are going to choose by a mile I also think that turning the table on the EU gangsters and playing hard ball would make her far more popular than she is right now because the vast majority of the British public have had a belly full of the EU and the way it has treated the UK since the vote to leave."

"If we did not pay our exit bill we would have £39 billion in the bank."

And here is a personal threat I received on social media just for fun

> Trying to make money from the UKs at with Brussels?
>
> I'll give you publicity.
>
> But not the sort you'll like.

Like · Reply · 23h   2

The EU don't need us more than we need them. I run a portfolio business. Supposing I juggle 10 clients and one of them decides they no longer want to work with me anymore. I lose notionally 10% of my business. Supposing that client is a good client and they are worth say 25%. I am upset but it does not kill me. I must work hard to make up the shortfall by seeking another client. It is the same with the EU 27.

Clearly some countries and industries are disproportionately affected. France, Belgium, Holland, Ireland and so on. The automotive industry etc. Precisely why we are seeing the EU making trade deals with Japan and so on to help offset losses. I would be sure they will offer economic assistance packages in the same way that our Government has offered sweeteners to companies such as Nissan to stay in the UK. That's how it works!

As regards not paying the exit bill there are two points here:

Why do we need to pay an exit bill at all? Well, most macro scale projects require up front commitments without which they would not happen. We have committed those payments and we must therefore pay them.

Why can't we just not pay? There are only two circumstances in your life when you can avoid paying a bill. When you never intend ever to trade with anyone ever again and when you are fixing to die. Trade relies on trust. If the UK does not settle its exit bill, our country's "Trust Pilot" score will be minus 300. It will set a toxic context for any trade deals we wish to strike in the future.

£39 billion sounds like a lot but it is just another trick using a one-sided argument. We need to "Go Compare". We have already spent considerably more than this getting nowhere on Brexit. It is not a small amount but it ignores what we get back for it and in the scheme of things it is not the largest sum of money we spend. For comparison, Brexit will have cost us £100 billion every year until 2030.

I can think if few good answers for the people who just want to bomb France. We are not at war last time I looked …

Sovereignty

Typical complaints include:

> *"We cannot even decide on the shape of our bananas."*
>
> *"I want my country back."*

Many but not all claims about sovereignty concern hypnotic inductions about Queen and country etc. These have been installed by our popular press over many decades. The fact that they are mostly untrue does not mean that if you disprove them, your subject will repent. Some of these beliefs are hardwired into the subject's heart and soul, rather like the Pavlovian response to stand up when the national anthem is played.

Perhaps the best strategy is to use the meta model to unpick which parts of their country they want back, and perhaps to listen carefully to their "story", getting them to highlight which aspects of the story are down to the EU, which our own Government and which down to general changes. There is a great deal of nostalgia built into the collage of reasons why people wanted to leave the EU.

The banana issue is a great opportunity to explain that they were lied to. If you get that far the next key move is to ask them hypnotically to wonder what other lies they have been told. Some will tell you that all politicians lie and almost suggest that it is an agreeable state of affairs. Lots of open-ended questions can help and a desire to leave your subject with more questions than answers can be a good strategy.

Democracy

On this thorny topic, Brexiteers typically say things like:

> *"We already had the final say in 2016."*

> *"It's anti-democratic to keep repeating a vote."*

> *"To run ourselves."*

> *"Are you against democracy?"*

> *"It was the only thing I've ever done where my voice counted. And you want to take that away from me."*

Firstly, the referendum is commonly thought to be binding when it is not. It clearly stated that it was an advisory referendum. At the same time David Cameron said he would abide by the result, which is where the confusion arises.

Typically, referenda that are binding require a 2/3 majority and are often conducted in stages. An initial vote on principles and another on practices for example.

In any case, democracy is a continuing process not a project with a single end point. If that were the case we would have never had the 2016 referendum in the first place as we had a referendum in 1975.

The 51.9% vote to leave comprised several major "segments", only the last one of which addressed the "exam question." The vote conflated these elements:

1. Those who wanted to "stick it to Cameron." Of course, David Cameron behaved atrociously, producing an appalling leaflet and campaign in general. Vote Leave's campaign was far superior in potency.

2. Those who were swayed by Nigel Farage's Nazi inspired "Breaking Point" poster. This created the illusion of "millions of immigrant invaders." It was supported by a campaign of fake news through targeted Facebook ads about Turkey being a member of the EU etc.

3. People who thought we would be getting £350 Million back every week for the NHS, from the advert on the side of a bus. Supported by a series of other trivial but potent lies such as Boris' bendy bananas etc.

4. And a group who wanted to leave the EU for a host of reasons, some imagined and others to do with perceived rule by a foreign entity and an unaccountable bureaucracy.

Mission Creep / EU Superstate

Typically, Brexiteers offer remarks like this:

"Germany and France run the EU, we don't have any say. It was supposed to be a trading arrangement only."

"Don't know anything about that, it was all done for Germany and we spent Billions on them after the war."

"It was our money, we give them money for nothing. It only helps Germany, out means out. We'll be alright. We survived the War, we can do it again!"

"We must escape the Nazis."

"It started as a trading thing. Now they want to interfere in our daily lives."

All organisations have mission creep. Nokia started life making toilet roll. 3M began by mining and now do Post-It Notes and so on. My hunch is that the main issue here is that the EEC started as a trading bloc and has now extended beyond that purpose. The UK has generally approved of EU decisions. Some 97% of EU decisions are approved of by our people. We have generally not agreed when it has not suited us and that's why we have the Pound, are not in Schengen and so on. As for the return on our investment, the best place to find out what the EU does for us is at www.myeu.uk

Oblivion / Self centeredness

Typically, Brexiteers say things like:

"It'll be alright", as I tell them I'll lose my home and job."

"We don't mean you. It's the other immigrants."

"I don't care about anyone else, my hoover is not powerful enough."

"All I care about is my health and social care."

One of the most difficult areas as you are trying to get your subject to care about things they clearly don't care about ...

One strategy is to play the scenario forward, pointing out how the things they care about will be affected. Sadly, this is usually met with the response "project fear." They must find out for themselves. If you are feeling brave you can confront the selfishness, asking them if there was ever a time when they needed others and so on.

Since they are likely to have low awareness of others, there is little point in trying to change that. Any change must come from finding ways to make them selfishly want to Remain in the EU.

Taking someone on a visit to a care home is a salutary experience as they suddenly gain a preview of their future and the fact that very few Brits work in such places.

Immigration

> *"Immigrants are stealing all our jobs because they push wages down."*

> *"If you love the EU so much, why don't you move there?"*

> *"They're comin' over'ere takin' are jobs."*

Immigration is another one of the most difficult areas as you are often dealing with irrational beliefs about people who appear to be different than the people who fear them. The term immigration is also loaded with sub-plots so it is difficult to offer a serious of algorithms to deal with all known victims of "Brexitosis". With some of the statements it is possible to supply facts if your subject is listening. For example, the illusion of immigrants taking jobs can be challenged quite easily if your subject listens.

I often point out that people do not leave their families to come to the UK. Many of them also do jobs that British people will not do for the wages on offer. In some cases they do jobs that we are not capable of doing, yet this shines the light on your subject's inadequacies and makes the conversation difficult.

Other areas of challenge include the fact that the data does not support the idea that immigrants take British jobs. As we know facts do not convince however.

Immigrants do not however push wages down. That comes down to our own Government, unscrupulous employers and supply and demand factors.

Myths and legends

Typically, Brexiteers say things like:

> *"Get rid of unelected bureaucrats."*

> *"Bring back King Arthur."*

> *"We must take back control."*

> *"I want sovereignty."*

Let's talk about BREX .. it

"Get on with it, we won."

"Stop bendy bananas."

"Trust me it's all fear mongering."

"You Remainers have no faith in the British people and think we are only great because of Germany and France."

"Bananas? We're going to grow our own."

"EU is collapsing."

"Oh, yeah … how's that turning out for Greece?"

Other

"If there's another vote I'm never going to vote again."

"I feel really sorry for Theresa May."

"Oh yes and Poor TM It's not her fault she's doing her best.'

"I actually don't understand any of it."

"You're all fear mongers."

"Brexit is an unmitigated disaster."

Followed by a personal story of devastation and often tears and hugs.

"Juncker is a piss artist."

.

"Brexit – what's this?"

"Get over it leave won."

"End off."

Let's talk about BREX .. it

"The same essperts what couldn't predict 2008!!"

"Err many did... they just don't write in The Sun ... and no one listened."
Oi wan' me sovrinty back!

Well, I leave you to your own Brexorcisms from here on ...

Acknowledgements

I am grateful to the following people for helping to provide the questions: Sarah Yoga, Maria Luisa, Lee Alexander, Ulrike Behrendt, John Castle, Chris Gamble, Grazia Valentino-Boschi, Annelles Schouppe, Mary Miraglia, Dimitri Seirlis, Barry Morgan, Karen Windahl Finnigan, Pieter Feld, Jaqueline Bridgeman, Rachel Ashley, Udo Keller, Sian Davies, Yvonne Wancke, Teresa Burton-Brown, Cathy Pearcy, Gail Caroline, Guillaumme Gee, John Laforge, Cliff Chapman, Chris Eden-Green, Helen Glanville.

Let's talk about BREX .. it

Reasons to be cheerful

350 reasons to Stop Brexit and stay in the EU

This is a splendid list from Paul Cawthorne.

EU AND BRITAIN'S GLOBAL ROLE

1. The EU has helped maintain peace in Europe for over 60 years
2. The UK has greater global influence as a member of the EU
3. Brexit would diminish, not enhance, the UK's global influence
4. The EU provides a counterweight to the global power of the US, Russia and China
5. Trump's "America First" isolationist, protectionist policies have weakened the UK's "special relationship" with the US
6. The UK's closest natural allies are now France, Germany and our other West European neighbours
7. The UK's global role is defined by its membership of the EU together with other international organisations including NATO, the UN Security Council, OECD, G7 and G20
8. No prominent UK political leaders or parties are advocating leaving any of these other global institutions
9. The UK worked together with other EU members in the Common Foreign and Security Policy (CFSP)
10. The EU has worked closely with NATO in enhancing European security
11. EU members have collaborated to support the Iran nuclear deal
12. EU members have imposed common sanctions on Russia since the annexation of the Crimea in 2014
13. EU security cooperation to combat piracy off Somalia

EU TRADE AND INVESTMENT

14. The EU is the world's largest trading bloc
15. The EU has over 500 million consumers
16. The EU represents 23% of global GDP
17. The EU accounts for 44% of all UK exports of goods and services
18. The EU accounts for 53% of all UK imports of goods and services

19. The UK enjoys tariff-free trade within the EU
20. The abolition of non-tariff barriers (quotas, subsidies, administrative rules etc.) among members
21. The EU never has been a "protectionist racket"
22. The EU is a springboard for trade with the rest of the world through its global clout
23. Participation in EU free trade agreement with Japan
24. Participation in EU free trade agreement with and Canada
25. Participation in EU free trade agreement with South Korea
26. Participation in EU free trade agreement with Mexico
27. Participation in EU free trade agreement with Chile
28. Participation in multilateral trade negotiations through EU membership of the WTO
29. Outside the EU the UK would have to renegotiate all its trade agreements
30. On average a free trade agreement takes at least 7 years to negotiate
31. As a member of the EU the UK maintains a say in the shaping of the rules governing its trade with its European partners
32. Brexit would leave the UK still subject to EU trading rules but no longer with any say in shaping them
33. UK trade with some countries in Europe has increased by as much as 50% as a result of EU membership.
34. Cheaper food imports from continental Europe
35. Cheaper alcohol imports from continental Europe
36. All major non-European trading powers are giving priority to trade with the EU as a whole, not the UK on its own
37. Potential future trade partners such as India and Turkey are likely to demand concessions on free movement in exchange for a trade deal
38. The net benefit of EU membership is at least £60 billion per year (CBI estimate)
39. The EU accounts for 47% of the UK's stock of inward Foreign Direct Investment (FDI), worth over $1.2 trillion
40. The UK's net contribution to the EU budget is around €7.3bn, or 0.4% of GDP (less than an eighth of the UK's defence spending)
41. The City of London, as a global financial hub, has acted as a bridge between foreign business and the EU

BENEFITS OF THE SINGLE MARKET

42. Investment flows across borders inside the EU have doubled since the introduction of the Single Market in 1993
43. The Single Market underpins access to European supply chains

44. Free movement of labour from the EU has overwhelmingly benefitted the UK economy
45. FDI into the UK has effectively doubled since the creation of the EU Single Market
46. Access to the EU Single Market has helped attract investment into the UK from outside the EU
47. No paper work or customs for goods throughout the Single Market
48. Tory Brexiteers have conveniently forgotten that Margaret Thatcher was a leading architect and supporter of the Single Market
49. British banks have been able to operate freely across the EU
50. British insurance companies have been able to operate freely across the EU
51. Long delays at ports and airports will occur if the UK leaves both the single market and customs union
52. The Single Market has brought the best continental footballers to the Premier League

HOW DOES THE UK BENEFIT FROM EU FUNDING?

53. 13% of EU budget earmarked for scientific research and innovation
54. The UK receives £730 million a year in EU funding for research
55. EU funding for UK universities
56. Potential damaging loss of Horizon 2020 research funding if the UK leaves the EU
57. Cornwall receives up to £750 million per year from the EU Social Fund (ESF)
58. £26m capital funding from the EU for the Eden project
59. £25m funding from the EU for Blackpool's tourist infrastructure and improved sea defences
60. £50 million EU funding towards the International Convention Centre and Symphony Hall in Birmingham
61. £450 million of EU funding destined to be spent on improving infrastructure on Merseyside in the period 2014 to 2020, including John Lennon airport and the cruise liner terminal
62. The Scottish Highlands, East Wales and Tees Valley are due to receive EU funding of over €300 per person in the period 2014-2020
63. 20,000 projects in the north of England received EU funding between 2007-2013 creating over 70,000 jobs
64. EU funding for the regeneration of Redcar seafront
65. EU funding for the Digital City in Middlesbrough
66. Structural funding for areas of the UK hit by industrial decline (South Wales, Yorkshire)

67. Support for rural areas under the European Agricultural Fund for Regional Development (EAFRD)
68. £122 million EU funding for the "Midlands engine" project
69. Financial support from the EU for over 3000 small and medium enterprises (SMEs) in the UK
70. EU funding for British sport, including football apprenticeships, tennis and rugby league
71. Access to the European Solidarity Fund in case of natural disasters
72. Since 1985 the UK has received a budget rebate equivalent to 66% of its net contribution to the EU budget
73. Leaving the EU would mean no more access to EU funding in many important areas

EU AND CONSUMER RIGHTS

74. Europe-wide patent and copyright protection
75. EU consumer protection laws concerning transparency and product guarantees of quality and safety
76. Under EU law consumers can send back a product bought anywhere in the EU if it breaks down within two years of purchase.
77. EU law prohibits misleading advertising
78. Improved food labeling
79. A ban on growth hormones and other harmful food additives
80. Cheaper air travel due to EU competition laws
81. Common EU maritime passenger rights
82. Common EU bus passenger rights
83. Deregulation of the European energy market has increased consumer choice and lowered prices
84. EU competition laws protect consumers by combatting monopolistic business practices
85. Strict controls on the operations of Multinational Corporations (MNCs) in the EU
86. Outside the EU there is no guarantee that a future UK government would maintain the current levels of consumer protection

EU AND LABOUR RIGHTS

87. Minimum paid annual leave and time off work (Working Time Directive)
88. Equal pay between men and women enshrined in European law since 1957
89. The right to work no more than 48 hours a week without paid overtime

90. Minimum guaranteed maternity leave of 14 weeks for pregnant women
91. Rights to a minimum 18 weeks of parental leave after child birth
92. EU anti-discrimination laws governing age, religion and sexual orientation
93. EU rules governing health and safety at work
94. The rights to collective bargaining and trade union membership are enshrined in EU employment law
95. Outside the EU a future UK government would be allowed to lower labour protection standards

EU AND EDUCATION

96. EU funding for UK universities
97. 46,000 EU nationals work in UK universities
98. The mutual recognition of professional qualifications has facilitated the free movement of engineers, teachers and doctors across the EU
99. The mutual recognition of educational diplomas
100. The Common European Framework of Reference for Languages (CEFR) has standardized assessment of language proficiency across the EU
101. The freedom to study in 28 countries (many EU universities teach courses in English and charge lower fees than in the UK)
102. The Erasmus programme of university exchanges (benefitting 16000 UK students a year)
103. Brexit would seriously compromise the rights and opportunities for the younger generation
104. Brexit is overwhelmingly opposed by people under 30
105. The Brexit referendum has divided many families between pro-EU younger generations and pro-Brexit parents and grandparents

EU AND THE ENVIRONMENT

106. The EU has played a leading role in combatting global warming (Paris 2015 climate change conference)
107. Common EU greenhouse gas emissions targets (19% reduction from 1990 to 2015)
108. Improvements in air quality (significant reductions in sulphur dioxide and nitrogen oxides) as a result of EU legislation
109. Reductions in sewage emissions
110. Improvements in the quality of beach water

111. Improvements in the quality of bathing water
112. EU standards on the quality of drinking water
113. EU targets to reduce water pollution in Britain's rivers
114. Restrictions on landfill dumping
115. EU targets for recycling
116. EU directive enforcing the use of unleaded petrol
117. Common EU regulations on the transportation and disposal of toxic waste
118. The implementation of EU policies to reduce noise pollution in urban areas
119. EU policies have stimulated offshore wind farms
120. EU support for solar energy
121. EU award of €9.3 million to Queens University Belfast for research into tidal and wave energy
122. EU promotion of the circular economy to enhance environmental sustainability
123. Outside the EU a future UK government would be free to lower environmental standards
124. Strict safety standards for cars, buses and trucks
125. Protection of endangered species and habitats (EU Natura 2000 network)
126. Strict ban on animal testing in the cosmetics industry

EU CITIZENS IN THE UK

127. More than 3 million citizens of the EU 27 are legally resident in the UK
128. The UK has never implemented the EU directive 2004/38/EC which allows EU member states to repatriate EU nationals after three months if they have not found the means to support themselves
129. Uncertainty about Brexit has caused a significant fall in net migration since the referendum
130. Free movement of labour has helped UK firms plug skills gaps (translators, doctors, plumbers)
131. 10% of doctors in the NHS are EU nationals
132. 7% of nurses in the NHS are EU nationals
133. 46,000 EU nationals work in UK universities
134. Free movement of labour has helped address shortages of unskilled workers (fruit picking, catering)
135. 28% of construction workers in London are from the EU
136. EU migrants make up 45 percent of the tourism and hospitality workforce
137. The retail industry has 170,000 people from the EU directly working for it, which accounts for 6% of the industry's UK workforce

138. The European Medical Agency (EMA) which employs 900 people is relocating to Amsterdam
139. The European Banking Authority (EBA) which employs 170 people is relocating to Paris
140. Uncertainty about Brexit has caused great anxiety and insecurity among the 3 million EU residents in the UK
141. Brexit threatens to provoke a brain drain of EU workers from the UK
142. There has been a rise in racial abuse and violent attacks since the referendum

UK CITIZENS IN THE EU

143. At least 1 million UK citizens live in the rest of the EU
144. 80% of these are below retirement age
145. British businesses, workers, pensioners and students have enjoyed huge benefits from freedom of movement inside the EU's Single Market over the last 30 years
146. The freedom to set up a business in 28 countries
147. The ability to retire in any member state
148. Pension transferability
149. The right to vote in local elections if resident in any member state
150. The right to vote in European Parliamentary elections if resident in any member state
151. There is currently no guarantee that UK residents in the EU will continue to enjoy their existing rights as EU citizens
152. Uncertainty about Brexit has caused great anxiety and insecurity among o UK residents in rest of the EU
153. Outside the EU there is no guarantee that British citizens would continue to enjoy access to healthcare on the same basis
154. Consular protection from any EU embassy outside the EU
155. The right to reside in any EU member state
156. The freedom to work in 28 countries without visa and immigration restrictions
157. The mutual recognition of professional qualifications has facilitated the free movement of engineers, teachers and doctors across the EU
158. The mutual recognition of educational diplomas

BENEFITS FOR BRITISH TOURISTS IN THE EU

159. No time-consuming border checks for travellers (apart from in the UK)

160. EU competition laws have facilitated the use of EasyJet, Ryanair and other low-cost airlines
161. The right to receive emergency healthcare in any member state (EHIC card)
162. EU laws making it easier for British people to buy second homes on the continent
163. The enhancement of price transparency
164. The removal of commissions on currency transactions across the Eurozone
165. Mutual recognition of the common European driving license
166. The introduction of the European pet passport
167. The abolition of mobile telephone roaming charges
168. Thanks to EU membership, Spain, Portugal and Greece have become major destinations for British tourists

EU DICTATORSHIP MYTH

169. The notion of an "EU dictatorship" is a commonly repeated Brexiteer myth
170. As a member of the EU the UK has never ceased to be "an independent sovereign nation"
171. The vast majority of the UK's laws are still decided by the Westminster parliament
172. The UK voluntarily agreed to share and pool sovereignty within the EU in many areas where collective action is more effective than decisions made at a national level (e.g. combatting climate change)
173. As a member of NATO, the UK has surrendered partial sovereignty in the interests of collective defence. This has never been opposed by the leading Brexiteers
174. The idea that the EU has a "democratic deficit" is only partially true
175. The most powerful EU institution is the European Council which includes the elected heads of national governments
176. The UK enjoys veto power in many important policy areas
177. The European Commission is fully accountable to the elected European Parliament
178. The European Parliament is elected every 5 years
179. The system of proportional representation for EP elections ensures a much broader and fairer representation than at Westminster (including UKIP and Green MEPs)
180. The EU has no more of a democratic deficit than the UK (unelected House of Lords) and the US (electoral college system)
181. The UK enjoys an opt out from the single currency

182. The UK maintains full control of its borders as an island nation and non-member of the Schengen area
183. Since 1985 the UK has received a budget rebate equivalent to 66% of its net contribution to the EU budget
184. Staying in the EU would not prevent a future Labour government from nationalising the railways or other public services
185. The EU helped support and maintain democracy in Spain, Portugal and Greece from the 1970s
186. The EU has helped support and maintain democracy in the ex-communist states of Eastern Europe since 1989

THERESA MAY AND THE CABINET IN THEIR OWN WORDS

187. Prime Minister Theresa May has never believed in the wisdom of Brexit
188. "I think being part of a 500m trading bloc is significant for us. I think one of the issues is a lot of people invest here in the UK because it's the UK in Europe". (Theresa May April 2016)
189. "It is not clear why other EU member states would give Britain a better deal than they themselves enjoy." (Theresa May April 2016)
190. "No country or empire in world history has ever been totally sovereign" (Theresa May April 2016)
191. "I do not want the people of Scotland to think that English Eurosceptics put their dislike of Brussels ahead of our bond with Edinburgh and Glasgow." (Theresa May, April 2016)
192. Outside the EU "London's position as the world's leading financial centre would be in danger." (Theresa May, April 2016)
193. "The only thing leaving the EU guarantees is a lost decade for British business)" (Sajid Javid, May 2016)
194. "None of our allies wants us to leave the EU – not Australia, not New Zealand, not Canada, not the US. In fact, the only country, if the truth is told, that would like us to leave the EU is Russia. That should probably tell us all we need to know." (Philip Hammond, March 2016)
195. "A strong NHS needs a strong economy – we should not put that at risk with Brexit" (Jeremy Hunt March 2016)
196. "The single market is essential to this government's agenda for trade and competitiveness." (David Lidington, 2010)
197. "Conservative Members believe in the Single Market because we believe profoundly in the importance of free trade and we want Europe to be at the centre of a free-trading world." (Liam Fox 2013)

BREXITEERS IN THEIR OWN WORDS

198. Leading Brexiteers have conveniently forgotten what they once said about the EU, the Single Market and the use of referendums
199. "A democracy that cannot change its mind ceases to be a democracy" (David Davis, 2012)
200. "We should not ask people to vote on a blank sheet of paper and tell them to trust us to fill in the details afterwards" (David Davis, 2002)
201. "You could have two referendums. As it happens, it may make more sense to have the second referendum after the negotiation is completed" (J.R. Mogg, 2011)
202. "I'm in favour of the single market. I want us to be able to trade freely with our European friends and partners." (Boris Johnson, 2013)
203. Leaving the single market would mean "…. diverting energy from the real problems of this country – low skills, social mobility, low investment…that have nothing to do with Europe." (Boris Johnson, Daily Telegraph, February 2016)
204. "Conservative Members believe in the Single Market because we believe profoundly in the importance of free trade and we want Europe to be at the centre of a free-trading world." (Liam Fox 2013)

LEAVE CAMPAIGN AND REFERENDUM

205. The 2016 referendum was advisory and not legally binding
206. The 2016 referendum took place without any preparation of how to proceed in the case of a Leave victory
207. The 2016 unfairly excluded two categories of people directly impacted by the result: EU citizens resident in the UK and long-term British residents abroad
208. The referendum made no provision for a "super majority" which is normal international practice when constitutional change is involved
209. The Leave EU campaign has been found to have violated electoral law
210. The Leave campaign violated an agreement to suspend campaigning after the murder of Jo Cox
211. The Leave campaign lied about £350 million a day becoming available for the NHS
212. The Leave campaign grossly exaggerated the threat of mass immigration (45% of Leave Facebook ads were on immigration)
213. The Leave campaign blatantly exploited xenophobia and anti-immigrant sentiment
214. The Leave campaign lied about Turkey joining the EU

215. The Leave campaign lied about a free trade deal with the EU being "the easiest thing in human history"
216. The Leave campaign deliberately misled the public by repeatedly stating that Brexit would not threaten Britain's place in the Single Market
217. The Leave campaign misled the public about the ease of signing trade agreements with the Commonwealth countries and other non-European partners
218. The referendum result was heavily influenced by a 20-year orchestrated anti-EU campaign led by pro-Brexit tabloid newspapers involving lies, xenophobic propaganda and smear tactics
219. Leading Brexiteers Arron Banks and Andy Wigmore had a series of undisclosed meetings with Russian officials during the referendum campaign
220. At the time of the referendum the majority of the public had little or no understanding of the workings of EU institutions (Council, Commission, Parliament etc)
221. At the time of the referendum the majority of the public had little or no understanding of the functioning of the EU Single Market
222. At the time of the referendum the majority of the public had little or no understanding of the functioning of the EU Customs Union
223. At the time of the referendum the majority of the public had little or no understanding of the jurisdiction of the European Court of Justice
224. At the time of the referendum the public were given little or no explanation of how the Article 50 procedure would work
225. The referendum was never about ordinary citizens "taking back control". It was a cynical and failed attempt to make peace within the Conservative Party
226. The Leave campaign slogan "take back control" was invented by a hypnotist
227. There is now a clear majority in favour of a referendum on the final Brexit deal with an option to remain in the EU

WHO WOULD REALLY BENEFIT FROM BREXIT?

228. Brexit is being driven by a radical right-wing agenda to create a deregulated economy with reduced labour, consumer and environmental protection
229. Brexit would stop the UK from implementing the EU's tax avoidance directive from 2019
230. Brexit would favour the economic interests of super rich Brexit backers who keep the majority of their assets offshore
231. The Leave campaign was supported and financed by a group of offshore super rich Brexiteers who looked to profit from the outcome ("the Bad Boys of Brexit")
232. Brexiteer John Redwood has advised investors to take their money out of the UK

233. Brexiteer Lord Ashcroft has advised UK businesses to set up in Malta
234. Brexiteer and Britain's richest man Sir James Radcliffe has just moved to Monaco
235. Major Leave campaign donor and hedge fund manager, Crispin Odey, has advised clients to prepare for a recession and higher inflation since the referendum

BREXIT WONT FIX IT!

236. 1. Leaving the EU is not the solution to any of Britain's social and economic problems
237. Leaving the EU will not reduce poverty in the UK
238. Leaving the EU is not the solution to growing inequality
239. Leaving the EU will not help reduce violent crime
240. Leaving the EU will not enhance environmental protection
241. Leaving the EU will not protect us from the impact of climate change
242. Leaving the EU will not improve the provision of healthcare in the NHS
243. Leaving the EU will not help solve the housing crisis
244. Leaving the EU will not help raise educational standards
245. By pursuing Brexit, the government has been paralyzed and has not unable to address any of these other issues
246. Leading Brexiteers have stopped arguing that Brexit will bring economic benefits and grudgingly accept the inevitably of short-term collateral damage
247. Jacob Rees Mogg has accepted that Brexit may not bring any tangible benefits for 50 years

THE FINANCIAL COSTS OF LEAVING

248. Leaving the EU involves paying a hefty divorce bill of £39 billion
249. The pound has lost 15% of its value since the referendum and is predicted to slide further if Brexit goes ahead
250. A devalued pound has already increased the price of continental holidays for British tourists
251. A further devaluation of the pound will cause rising food prices and higher inflation
252. The devaluation of the pound has increased the purchase price of second homes in the Eurozone
253. The devaluation of the pound has reduced the real value of pensions for UK residents in the EU 27

254. Economic growth in the UK is now the lowest in the G7 having slowed dramatically since the referendum
255. The UK economy has lost up to £35 billion in output over the last two years
256. Real wages have been falling since the referendum
257. The government's own Brexit impact reports have predicted a negative economic effect in the event of any Brexit scenario
258. The government has attempted to conceal the findings of its negative impact studies
259. The government's divisions and negotiating incompetence has increased the risk of a catastrophic No Deal Brexit
260. A No Deal Brexit would create a hole of £80 billion in the public finances according to Chancellor Philip Hammond
261. According to the government's own studies a No Deal Brexit is expected to have a catastrophic effect on 84 vital areas of British life
262. The fact that the government is even feeling the need to prepare for a No Deal scenario reveals the bankruptcy of its approach

BREXIT AND JOB LOSSES

263. 3.1 million jobs in the UK are directly linked to exports to the EU
264. Over 70,000 retail jobs have disappeared since the referendum, and the pace of losses has accelerated in the past year.
265. Construction has also suffered, with 17,000 jobs disappearing in the year until March 2018
266. Potential for manufacturing job losses if UK based firms feel the need to relocate to the EU27
267. Uncertainty about Brexit is already threatening jobs in the UK car industry
268. Airbus, which employs 14,000 workers in the UK, has threatened to move production out of the country
269. BMW which employs 7,000 workers in the UK, has threatened to move production out of the country
270. Panasonic are moving their European headquarters from London to Amsterdam
271. The City of London is predicted to lose at least 5,000 jobs in the financial sector

THE NEW WILL OF THE PEOPLE

272. The electorate has changed since June 2016 with new young voters overwhelmingly opposed to Brexit

273. Future demographic trends will continue to augment support for EU membership
274. Opinion polls since the beginning of 2018 have consistently indicated that a majority of the public are now opposed to Brexit
275. A comprehensive YouGov study has found that 112 constituencies would now shift from Leave to Remain
276. The majority of voters in Wales would now support remaining in the EU
277. Two thirds of Scottish voters (66%) now support EU membership, compared to 62% in June 2016
278. The majority of small companies (56%) would now vote to remain in the EU
279. Refusing to recognise that the new "will of the people" is to stop Brexit is a negation of democracy

TAKING OUR COUNTRY BACK?

280. Support for Brexit has been based on a false nostalgia to "take our country back" to a better world that never existed
281. In the early 1970s before Britain joined the EC average life expectancy was 10 years lower than today
282. Before the UK joined the EC 20% of children left school with no qualifications
283. In 1973 only 15% of young people attended university
284. In 1973 inflation was nearly 10%
285. In 1973 the UK economy was considered the "sick man of Europe" with living standards 7% below the EC average
286. Britain was definitely not a better place in the early 1970s before we joined the EU
287. The supposed benefits of Brexit are based on wishful thinking, delusions of grandeur and a misrepresentation of history and economic reality

BREXIT CAN BE REVERSED

288. Brexit is not, and has never been, a "done deal"
289. Article 50 is reversible. Brexit is not inevitable
290. Article 50 was activated prematurely without any coherent agreed government plan for leaving the EU
291. The decision to trigger Article 50 without a clear plan was like "putting a gun in your mouth and pulling the trigger." (Leave campaign director, Dominic Cummings, May 2018)

292. None of the EU27 is opposed to the UK reversing Brexit
293. There is no majority in parliament for a soft Brexit
294. There is no majority in parliament for a hard Brexit
295. There is no majority in parliament a no deal Brexit
296. There is no majority in parliament for any form of Brexit
297. The government is hopelessly divided about how to proceed with Brexit
298. The government's Chequers proposals will not be accepted by the EU
299. The government's Chequers proposals have been rejected by a large minority of MPs within the governing Conservative Party
300. The government's parliamentary majority is wafer thin and is just a few votes away from a catastrophic parliamentary defeat and political crisis this Autumn
301. The government's pro-Brexit parliamentary majority continues to rely on a shady deal with the extreme ultra-conservative DUP
302. 69% of the population of Northern Ireland now favour remain, compared to 56% in the 2016 referendum
303. The EU negotiators continue hold all the cards and are stalling for time, waiting to see if the government survives the Autumn

THE EU AND NORTHERN IRELAND

304. The EU acts as a guarantor of the Irish Good Friday Agreement
305. Since 1998 the EU has provided more than 1.5 billion euros in funding for Northern Ireland peace projects
306. A frictionless Irish border
307. Leaving the EU Customs Union would lead to a hard Irish border
308. It is a Brexiteer myth that Switzerland and Norway have an open border with the EU
309. Leaving the EU could compromise peace in Northern Ireland
310. Leaving the EU could hasten the breakup of the UK by stimulating support for a united Ireland
311. The government's pro-Brexit parliamentary majority continues to rely on a shady deal with the extreme ultra-conservative DUP
312. 69% of the population of Northern Ireland now favour remain, compared to 56% in the 2016 referendum

A Better Britain IN a Better Europe For a Better World

GIBRALTAR AND THE FALKLAND ISLANDS

313. The EU acts as a guarantor of the special status of Gibraltar
314. 97% of Gibraltar's residents voted to remain in the EU
315. Brexit would encourage Spain to press for a modification of Gibraltar's sovereign status
316. Leaving the Single Market would seriously damage the economy of the British Falkland Islands (94% of fish exports go to the EU)
317. Leaving the EU is likely to encourage Argentina to renew its claims over the Falkland Islands

About the person who wrote the 350 reasons to stay in the EU

Paul Cawthorne graduated from the London School of Economics in 1982. He became a poll tax exile in 1989 when he left the UK to live on the continent. Over the last 30 years he has worked as an economics and history teacher in national and international schools in the UK, France, Italy and Switzerland.

He is currently working as a "frontaliero" living in the north of Italy and commuting daily across the decidedly not "frictionless" border into Switzerland. Thanks to his daily experience stuck in border traffic he now considers himself to be an "expert" on leaving the EU.

Paul is married with two children.

WHO THINKS BREXIT IS A GOOD IDEA?

318. Brexit has been consistently opposed by the overwhelming majority of leading economists
319. Brexit has been consistently opposed by the overwhelming majority of leading environmentalists
320. Brexit has been consistently opposed by the overwhelming majority of leading scientists
321. Brexit is opposed by the BMA and the overwhelming majority of NHS doctors
322. Brexit is opposed by the Royal College of Nursing and the overwhelming majority of NHS nurses
323. Brexit is opposed by the overwhelming majority of Britain's trade unions
324. None of the other EU member state are considering leaving the EU
325. Even the Eurosceptic governments in Italy, Hungary and Poland support continued EU membership
326. No other EU member state is likely to leave the EU in the foreseeable future
327. Not a single democratically-elected head of government, apart from Trump, has publicly expressed support for Brexit
328. Brexit is favoured by all of the EU's extreme right-wing xenophobic parties including the French National Front, Italian Lega Nord and Dutch PVV
329. Brexit is "the stupidest thing any country has ever done" (Michael Bloomberg, October 2017)

SCIENCE, HEALTH AND RESEARCH INSIDE THE EU

330. 13% of EU budget earmarked for scientific research and innovation
331. The UK receives £730 million a year in EU funding for research
332. EU funding for UK universities
333. Potential damaging loss of Horizon 2020 research funding if the UK leaves the EU
334. UK participation in the EU Galileo satellite system
335. UK participation in the EU's Copernicus, the world's largest single earth observation programme
336. Membership of the European Medicines Agency (EMA) which monitors the quality and safety of medicines
337. Cooperation in the peaceful use of nuclear energy as a member of Euratom
338. Leaving the EU without a deal would lead to severe shortages of foods and medicines

POLICING AND SECURITY

339. EU cross-country coordination in Europol offers greater protection from terrorists, paedophiles, people traffickers and cyber-crime
340. The European common arrest warrant
341. Britain would lose influence on cross-border policing and security by leaving Europol after Brexit

CULTURAL BENEFITS OF EU MEMBERSHIP

342. EU membership has helped facilitate intercultural dialogue
343. Membership of the EU has helped revolutionise eating habits for many people in the UK
344. Minority languages such as Welsh and Irish are recognized and protected under EU law
345. EU funding for the British film industry
346. EU funding for British theatre, music and dance
347. Glasgow (1990) and Liverpool (2008) benefitted from being European capitals of culture, stimulating their local economies
348. UK membership of the EU has promoted the use of the English language which has replaced French as the EU's lingua franca

HUMAN RIGHTS IN THE EU

349. Human Rights protected under the EU Charter of Fundamental Rights
350. The death penalty can never be reintroduced as it is incompatible with EU membership

Let's talk about BREX .. it

Useful links

Rage Against the Brexit Machine

Website: www.brexitrage.com

Facebook: www.facebook.com/brexitrage
                            www.facebook.com/groups/RATBM

YouTube: www.youtube.com/academy-of-rock.co.uk "Politics and Business"

Twitter: @brexitrage @academyofrock

iTunes / Amazon / Google Play: Search on Google with the terms Rage Against the Brexit Machine iTunes etc.

End the Chaos: Gina Miller's project www.endthechaos.co.uk

The European Movement: Started by Winston Churchill and the oldest organisation that supports a united Europe www.europeanmovement.co.uk

Poems Against the Brexit Machine: A collective book of poetry to reach people's hearts www.brexitrage.com

Voices for Europe: A pan Remain group aimed at bringing together the disparate Remain groups www.voicesforeurope.com

Reasons to Remain: An excellent daily blog on the upsides of the EU written by Jon Danzig www.reasons2remain.co.uk

Let's talk about BREX .. it

EU Flag Mafia: A grass roots organisation that systematically surprises our Government with unusual stunts www.euflagmafia.com

SODEM: Daily protests outside Parliament www.sodemaction.co.uk

Europa United: A Pan European blogging site www.europaunited.eu

New Europeans: New Europeans is a campaigning group founded by Roger Casale www.neweuropeans.net

The New European: A newspaper dedicated to a Better Britain in a Better Europe for a Better World www.theneweuropean.co.uk

Best for Britain: Looking for the best options for a future Britain www.bestforbritain.co.uk

My EU: Find out what the EU has done in your area www.myeu.uk

Britain For Europe: Grassroots campaigning group www.britainforeurope.org

Printed in Great Britain
by Amazon